AF305148

ULYSSES S. CAT

and Other Animals
I Have Known

ULYSSES S. CAT

and Other Animals
I Have Known

SCOTT SIMON

LINE DRAWINGS BY
LIANA FINCK

W. W. NORTON & COMPANY

Independent Publishers Since 1923

For Caroline, Elise, and Paulina,
and our running mates through life

Some people talk to animals. Not many
listen though. That's the problem.

—A. A. MILNE, *WINNIE-THE-POOH*

ULYSSES S. CAT
and Other Animals I Have Known

INTRODUCTION

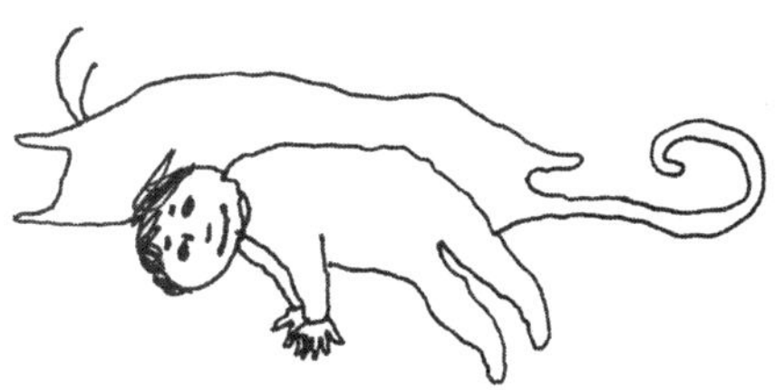

We don't make much of a distinction in our family between humans and the other animals. Two legs or four, flesh-covered, feathered, fur-covered, gilled or under a shell, we're all family. We coddle, confide in, and confess to our pets. They seek out, beseech, and comfort us. We read each other's minds, whims, angers, hungers, and anxieties. We share sleep, joys, sorrows, and untold hours of just staring—at the sky, into screens, or at one another. They nap in our sweaty clothing. We can pick up and appraise their droppings, like rare finds from an ancient dig. We bathe, comb, and bestow nicknames on our pets, and sing them silly songs that become family anthems. And we hold onto one another, often through their last breaths.

As I write these words, we have a French poodle named Daisy, a foster cat we call Gato Blanco, and a hamster named Bagel all in residence in our apartment, along with our two daughters. And oh, a bin on our balcony with about a thousand worms (they have been named "the Slimons"), wriggling and mulching, whom you might not think of as pets, but I know that when we pop the top of their slime-filled château to plop in kitchen scraps, my wife, Caroline, sings out to them, "Hello, my dear, dear slimy ones!" in a voice so sweet that Daisy growls, as if to say, "Hey! That's the voice she saves for me!" Our daughters are also widely employed in our neighborhood to care for animals. One customer is a man who arranges for his dog to be conveyed out of and into his building in a baby carriage. And alongside our pets, the floors of our apartment are dotted with the disemboweled bodies of small plush pigs, rams, alpacas, and zebras, which our dog and cat have eviscerated in their incessant search for the little squeeze toys sewn inside them.

Alerts go off in our lives every few hours, every day. Time to feed Daisy! Time for her walk! Time to put out fresh kibble for Gato! Check his cat box! What's going on with that one in the corner? The color is a little . . . off. Who can walk Daisy? She's scratching the door! She really needs to go! Wait, wait, don't forget the green bags! Oh, back, good. Almost time for her afternoon meal. But not quite yet—or she'll expect it at four every day! Wait, where's Gato? Did you turn your back when you opened the balcony door to check on the worms? Wait— there he is! On the piano! What's that sound? Is Bagel jogging? When did you change out his litter? Wait—Daisy is staring into Bagel's crate like it's the pain au chocolat case at a bakery . . .

And we imagine the alerts that go off in the minds of our pets. Hey, she's opened an eye! Time to walk walk walk! Hey, he's up up up! He's gonna stuff his face with leftovers and spill crumbs! Time to scamper into position! Hey, where'd she go? I was just napping, and—wait! I hear her in the kitchen! Let me be sure!

We do not call our pets our *fur babies*, but we almost reaffirm the term as we reach down to pet them, ruffle their fur, or carry them downstairs. And so how to describe the family ties we feel? *Owners* sounds cold; and it doesn't disclose the scores of different kinds of care that go back and forth between us. There is the current cliché of *caregivers*, but that suggests something one-sided and custodial. It does not describe what we enjoy when we dish out food and pats, and our pets respond with licks, hugs, and huge, imploring eyes. Maybe the Australian *mates*, or *compadres* in Spanish, might come closer to what we feel.

Gertrude Stein once wrote that she learned the rhythms of sentences and paragraphs by listening to her poodle, Basket, lap water from his bowl. I do believe our poodle, Daisy, and all the animals in our lives, can rank with Basket as a spring of inspiration. Pets unlock our hearts. They can make monarchs stoop to pat them, toddlers try to stand to touch them, and scholars babble to make them smile. Pets make us laugh, and produce memories we stow away for all time. The animals who share our lives can be direct as a lick, blunt as a bite, honest as a howl, and shameless as they scratch their most private parts. The pure, unequivocal love our animals call out in us is in our voices when we speak to them, in our hands as we touch them, and ultimately, in our tears and hopes to see them again when all our mortal lives have run out.

PENNY

I was born into a family who had a dog waiting. We've framed the first holiday card my parents sent out to friends and family when I was about nine months old: plump and plum-cheeked, plopped onto a couch with thin dark hair flipped up like a duckling's—and smiling. And what was there not to smile about? I was fed, changed, bathed, and with every whim catered to by the lovely Irishwoman who was my mother. I was tickled, spoiled, and utterly entertained professionally by my father, who was a comedian.

The face next to mine was large-eyed, interested, furry, and kind. It was Penny, our German shepherd, then in her late puppy phase. My parents scrawled across the card "Some Simon's are cute!!" I'm pretty sure they meant Penny.

Penny and I actually figured into the same family anecdote before I was even born. My mother was beginning to display evidence of my impending arrival on a night when my parents were to meet friends at a restaurant in Chicago's Lit-

tle Italy. But they did not want to leave Penny on her own in their apartment, where they figured from experience that she would whimper, chew the sofa, and gnaw table legs in anxiety. They thought. Then my father handed my mother a pair of sunglasses.

"Wear these," he said, and put a leash on Penny.

They must have been quite a sight when they entered the family-run Italian restaurant. My mother was a glamorous brunette, visibly pregnant, and outwardly blind, clinging to the arm of her devoted husband, preceded by her devoted guide dog.

"You could hear people gasp all over the restaurant," my mother would recall. "'Look at that blind young pregnant woman!' they'd say. 'So beautiful. So sad. But say, aren't those guide dogs supposed to be trained a little better than that?'"

My parents were seated at a long table with friends. Penny took up her position at my mother's feet. But when a platter of braciole or farro mafaldine was carried out from the kitchen, Penny would lurch, tongue lapping, nose quivering. "Oh, it's so beautiful!" my mother would gush from behind her sunglasses. "Yes, dear," my father would admonish for all the other diners to hear. "The food *sounds* beautiful, doesn't it?" Out would come bowls of spaghetti al nero di seppia, and shanks of osso buco. Penny would whimper loudly to be shunted under the table. My mother and father would hold onto her between whatever bites they could manage. "Good dog. Good *guide* dog!" my father would announce. "My beautiful Penny," my mother cooed. "She is telling me how *beautiful* the food is! How *lovely* it *looks*!"

The owner of the restaurant came over to my parents. "You're not really blind, are you?" he said.

"We couldn't leave her in our apartment," my mother admitted. "She's just a baby," and the restaurant owner smiled as diners began to call out, "Aww, let the poor pooch stay!"

"Just keep her out of the way," the owner told my parents. "Any problems, we're tight with the health department inspectors."

I soon came into the world, and my mother liked to recall that Penny's face—not hers; not my father's—was the first visage

I reached up from the crib to touch. She also said that I commenced to crawl only after Penny pushed my small, diapered backside with her nose, and that I began to stand and totter only after tugging myself into the land of the upright by the longest black and bronze hairs under Penny's neck. Yes, you could say that Penny raised me.

When I tugged down hard on her ear, just to see if it stayed put, or pulled on her tail, just to tell her I was around, this dog of a breed famed for its service with warriors and security officers would just whimper and put her nose against my cheek, softly.

Penny came to my parents through my grandfather, Sergeant Francis Lyons, CPD, Shakespeare District, Humboldt Park, who worked with police in the canine unit. They would often try to find homes for young German shepherds who, for one reason or another, didn't pass the police training regimen. Of course, the thought of this made Penny only more appealing to my parents.

"I'm sure they'd tell her, 'Go, Penny, chase down that bad guy!'" my mother said. "'He just robbed a bank!' And Penny, you know Penny, she loves everyone. She probably just thought, 'Well, he looked nice to me!'"

My father had a taxing schedule in those times. He was up at 5 a.m. to walk Penny, and then went to appear on an early-morning radio show. He'd come home, open a bottle, play with me, and nap until it was time to arise for a noontime comedy show. Flush with applause from a midday audience, he'd return to our apartment, make funny noises to amuse me, hear my mother's review of his performance (invariably gushing), inhale another shot of Early Times, walk Penny around the block, and nap until he had to leave for a 6 p.m. show under the marquee of the State-Lake Theater. He'd close out the workday with the Chez Show at the Chez Paree nightclub, where he warmed up conventioneers and tourists to applaud the likes of Mel Tormé, Sarah Vaughan, Nat King Cole, Jerry Lewis, and Tony Bennett. Then he'd stop for a drink—"to unwind"—and return to our apartment to unwind some more. He'd look in on me and my mother, then settle in with the bottle and Penny at his side.

You may notice a pattern. But while my mother was beginning to ask, "Do you really need another drink, dear? How many bottles have I seen this week?" Penny was his silent partner. We don't have to offer explanations to our pets.

One early morning, with the sun still asleep below the line of Lake Michigan, my father walked Penny along empty streets. She began to pull as they neared a hedge around an apartment building. My father pulled her back, then decided to heed Penny's urgency, and followed her to the edge of the hedge. He saw a pair of bare feet, leading up to the body of a woman in a pale nightgown. My father called out softly. There was no answer. Penny sniffed and licked. My father got to his knees and saw a face, still, and anything but peaceful.

My father and Penny then ran a half block up where they thought they might see a police cruiser, and flagged one down within a few moments. "My dog found a body!" my father told them. "She sniffed it out!"

The police officers turned up the street, approached the hedge carefully, and encountered what turned out to be the body of a North Side woman who had jumped to her death. The police patted and congratulated Officer Penny. "We can use her down at the station," they said.

My father and Penny returned to share the news of their adventure. "She was like Rin Tin Tin!" he enthused, citing a children's western starring a German shepherd and her boy on the old frontier. "I couldn't hold her back, I tell you!" I think my father was beginning to see possibilities for a new series: *Rin Tin Penny.*

But my father had a morning comedy gig, too, and by the time he was on his second show of the day and third or fourth drink, the afternoon newspapers had run the story, but said only something like, "The body was found by a man walking his dog." My mother recalled my father, Penny's snout resting on one knee, Early Times on another, calling the overnight desk of a couple of newspapers to admonish them, "Well, I am *that man*, and I tell you that *our dog*, Penny, *found* that body!" News accounts were not revised, but Penny retained top billing on our family marquee.

When I was old enough to crawl but not yet sold on walking, I would hold onto Penny with my small, chubby hands and try to get her to drag me along on her travels. She often turned to sniff and lick me, as if to caution, "No rush now. Just enjoy that spot on the floor. It's all yours." My parents would sometimes prop me, cowboy-style, atop Penny's neck. I can still recall feeling her stalwart muscles under my baby-fat butt. And I'd press into her, hug her thick coat of doggy-hairs, burrow my nose into her doggy-smell, and tickle my chin against her doggy-hairs. My good-night kisses came in threes: Mama, Dada, Penny. As I began to speak, I mouthed an *m-m-m* sound for Mama, a *d-d-d* sound for Dada, and *p-p-p* for Penny. I don't believe I thought that Penny was human, like me, my mother, my father, and my grandparents, but I knew that Penny was no less a member of the world that was our family.

My maternal grandmother, Frances Julia Sullivan Lyons, who was married to my grandfather, Sergeant Francis Joseph Lyons, CPD, seemed to have a particular closeness with Penny, too. When we went to their apartment, my grandmother would have a cocktail shaker, beaded with frosty droplets, waiting for my father, cookies for me, and some kind of bone for Penny. Frances was an elegant woman, who was a hostess at the Cape Cod Room in the Drake Hotel during the week (and funneled busboy, maid, maintenance, and server jobs to Sullivans and Lyons freshly arrived from Belfast). She'd get down on her knees on the rug in their front room, pearls brushing the floor, silvery hair tousled, and tug on the bone with Penny. "Thatta girl!" she'd encourage her. "That's my good girl!"

Our family arrived in the middle of the afternoon on Thanksgiving. It was quiet in their West Side neighborhood of three-story flats, and Chicago blustery. My mother rang the bell. No answer. Penny began to bark. My father had to draw back on her leash.

My mother turned the key. My father charged ahead and saw my grandmother's shoes on the floor, below a piano bench, family photos where sheet music should be. "Oh Jesus," he said, then commanded, "Stay there, Scotty," as my mother and Penny sprang forward. I remember seeing a yellow kitchen wall, a screaming bright overhead light, and the smell of Thanksgiving dinner. I remember hearing my mother gasp, "Oh mother . . ." to her own.

I stayed behind, because I think I was scared by whatever was ahead. I heard my father wrench open a window, and felt a gust of November. My mother rushed out to hold me. "Granny. She's gone, baby." I did not understand what she meant, and I think I really didn't want to know. My grandfather then arrived—my grandmother had sent him out on a sudden errand, to be alone as she undertook what she had decided to do—and I remember him holding a small brown wrinkled sack, his face reddening, his eyes swelling, then sobbing as the weight of what had happened fell on his shoulders.

Police in blue uniforms arrived, quiet and respectful.

It was a "blue family," as they said. My mother held onto me on a sofa, kissing my head. "Granny loved you . . . so much. So much, my baby . . ." My grandfather spoke to officers in a low voice I couldn't quite hear, and had never heard before. My father was in the kitchen, where there were sad, practical things to be done. And Penny stayed steadfastly by my grandmother. She looked on, said my father, sitting on her haunches, murmuring, mewling, sometimes leaning in to press her nose on my grandmother, softly.

There were blinking lights, but no sirens. Men in black coats, speaking softly, arrived with a stretcher. They covered my grandmother as they took her out through the front room. My mother held me in her arms as she put a kiss on her mother's fingers and touched the shape of her head as she went by. Penny trotted just under the stretcher, through a hallway, down the rise of stairs, and out into the street, looking on as the police closed the door on the person who gave her bones and played with, kissed, and gushed over her. "Ah, that's a good dog," said the officers. "One of our own. A great dog."

There is a brief recitation of circumstances to try to explain why my grandmother, who was just forty-four, decided to do what she did, to herself and her family, though of course no explanation made it more comprehensible to those who had to carry her loss like an untreated wound. Frances felt trapped in a sour marriage by the edicts of her faith. She had a succession of boyfriends (I know: the term is hilariously naïve) who were also married. My mother came to feel that this was to her mother's liking, until, perhaps, there was one married man who may have changed her feelings but did not want to change whatever congenial arrangement he supposed he had with my grandmother. My mother came to feel that Frances had sent my grandfather out on an errand (for a bottle of scotch they scarcely lacked) only so that he could return, discover her under the bench, and save her as the rest of us arrived. The turkey was already baked, browned, and resting on top of the stove.

"Granny drank, smoked, and played with fire," my mother told me when I was older. "I think she didn't think it through and just burned herself down."

My grandfather announced his engagement just a month later to a woman who was a typist at their station house. She had three burly brothers, also Irish, who informed my grandfather that he had a choice between marrying their sister and a life in traction. I remember my parents sorting out the news as they sat on swings in the backyard of our apartment building. My mother balanced me on her lap, and Penny was at my father's knee. People in families can know when to take up their positions.

"Frances isn't even cold in her grave," said my father. I remember Penny whimpering under my father's gentle hand.

"Penny misses her so," said my mother. "How do we explain what happened to Penny?"

What I see now is how the animals in our lives can help us

steer through a tangle of choking emotions. My parents felt misgivings, guilt, anger, and confusion over what my grandmother had done. Penny felt only her loss. Our dog's soft moans and close steps alongside Frances's stretcher helped keep open their hearts.

My father lost one job, then another. He tried one program to stop drinking, then another. He wound up taking a job in San Francisco, and our family wound up taking a cross-country train, but without Penny. My mother, father, and I would have to huddle in a small hotel room until we could rent an apartment. And so it was arranged for Penny to spend a few weeks in the green suburbs of Chicago, with the family of our dentist. They had an expansive home with a basement, a leafy backyard, and several children.

"It'll be a vacation for Penny," said my mother.

"Our detective dog deserves it," my father agreed.

When we had settled in San Francisco, the dentist and their family would drive west, see mountains and monuments, and deliver Penny.

My mother, father, and I rode cable cars, saw Fisherman's Wharf and North Beach, where my father was going to work. My mother took me to play each day in new parks, and she'd tell me, "Penny will love this. We can't wait until Penny is here."

My father and I were watching cartoons from the bed in our hotel room one night when my mother answered the phone, listened, and looked stricken. My father brought himself up, and she held out a hand. "Penny," she faintly whispered, tenderly, almost reverently.

It seems that Penny had been chasing after a car, as suburban dogs do. Something happened. The friendly dentist rushed her to a vet's office, but Penny was gone. He sobbed on the phone. "Well, it wasn't your fault," my mother told him. "She was a frisky, happy dog. I'm sure she had fun with you . . ." and my mother struggled as she spoke, until she could no longer hold herself back. I had seen my mother laugh, whistle, and sing, get angry, be astonished, and joke through so much. I couldn't recall ever seeing her cry. She had held herself back through so much. But the animals we love can take the guardrails off our hearts.

HOPPY

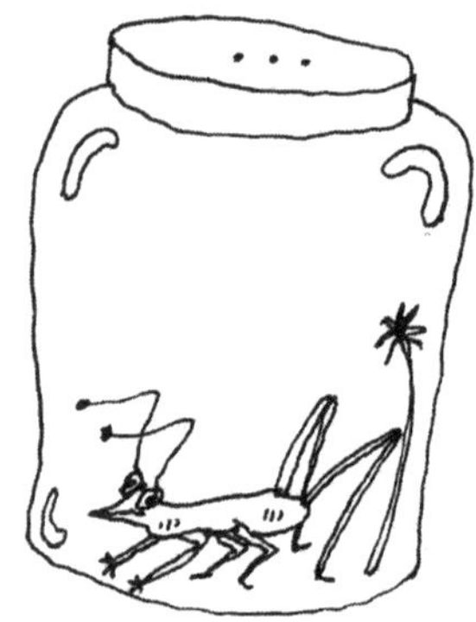

I didn't have another pet for most of my childhood. I lived with my aunt, uncle, and cousins for second grade, as my parents got divorced. My mother worked as a receptionist during the day and at nightclubs at night, while my father tried counseling, hospitals, doctors, programs, and various heralded therapies to stop drinking. He never could.

My aunt and uncle brought a dog into the family, a handsome and spirited Siberian husky called Troika, who had a ruffled collar of white hair that shimmered like a snow slide. Troika would chase me down hallways, to many giggles. But then he encountered a neighbor's gentle ginger cat one afternoon. The result was quick, one-sided, and unnerving. Troika was given a new home at a frat house at a local college. I like to think his high spirits and undomesticated appetites found more felicitous surroundings.

I spent most of my childhood years that followed going back and forth between the one-bedroom apartment I shared with my mother on Chicago's North Side and my father's single room in an old residence hotel. I was the only child of my parents, and the only child anyone saw at the St. Clair hotel, which had become a kind of way station for hoofers, lounge singers, and comics, like my father, who were between jobs, and often, also like my father, divorced, down in life, and drinking at all hours.

I know now there were also professional women working there. Mary Jo, Marlene, and a few more who fluffed my mousy brown hair with long red fingernails and laughed to see me blush, cherry red. There was also a retired mob gunsel in residence ("Too old to aim right," my father told me) named Frankie who would meet me in the blaring Hopper-bright diner downstairs on summer afternoons when I came back from day camp, and buy me hot fudge sundaes. Perhaps because he couldn't talk that much about himself, Frankie listened intently to all my stories about baseball games, playing capture the flag, and how Bruce tricked Gary into stepping on a dog turd. "Really?" he'd ask, eyes growing wide, as perhaps they once did for Sam Giancana. Frankie would pat my shoulder as I ran off from our sundaes and instruct my father, "Take care of that boy, Ernie." My father would reach for the skies. "I will, Frankie!" he vowed. "I promise!"

It was into these surroundings one day that I brought home Hoppy.

I'd been on a Friday night "campout." This amounted to about twenty boys in shorts eating hot dogs on blankets on the grass of the outfield of the baseball field of our camp, then singing "Michael, Row the Boat Ashore" and "Kumbaya" until we flapped crumbs off the blankets and fell asleep in right-center field, listening to the White Sox-Yankees game. City kids roughing it in the wilderness along Clark Street.

Saturday morning, I saw a grasshopper by the corner of my sleepy head. I brought my face close. He seemed to glow almost neon green, with small, soft brown pinpoint eyes, forelegs slender and tender-looking as blades of grass. He had two legs aft, thick as matchsticks and springy as rubber bands, and two, wiry, fragile-looking antennae over his fragile dot eyes.

His antennae twitched. Was he speaking—to me?

Impulsively, I gathered the grasshopper and some grass on which he perched into my empty tin lunchbox. When I returned to room 12M of the St. Clair, in which I lodged with my father, I popped open the top of the lunchbox and announced, "Meet Hoppy."

Hoppy seemed snug enough in his billet of grass. My father looked incredulous and slightly horrified. "You can't . . ." he began to sputter. "I mean . . . how will you . . . how will we . . . what will we . . . ?" He called my mother. I heard her laughter from across our small room, and watched my father's face as he struggled to absorb the advice that followed. "Uh-huh . . . so then we . . . well, I don't know where we . . ." We took Hoppy in his traveling conveyance downstairs to the hotel diner. Clark, who worked the counter, smiled, happy to be enlisted. He found an empty, tall, rinsed glass jar and put his hands in a scoop under my own to lift Hoppy from the lunchbox into his new digs. Clark threaded the top closed. "But Hoppy, he's got to breathe," he noted, and found a screwdriver in a thicket of kitchen cutlery. "Here we go," he said, and punched one, two, five, and six holes into the tin top of the jar.

Hoppy sat between me and my father at Clark's counter as we marked the occasion with grilled cheese sandwiches.

But Hoppy's diet soon became a worry. My father observed that he didn't seem to snack much on the grass I'd brought along and decreed that the blades of grass below Hoppy's hind legs must have turned dry and unappetizing.

It was Monday morning. We were in the midst of concrete towers, streets, and sidewalks. Greenery in downtown Chicago then was mostly the dill pickle and a sprig of parsley served alongside a deli sandwich. Lincoln and Grant Park were scores of blocks away. The Outer Drive (now named DuSable Lake Shore Drive) had slender "islands" of grass between north- and southbound traffic lanes, but traffic was unrelenting. Then my father spoke up.

"There is that bank at the corner," he reminded me. "Potted palms. They're green, aren't they?"

My father clipped on a tie and told me he'd soon return. Then he walked half a block over and cased the bank. There seemed to be more than a dozen thick-leaved palm plants (banana palms, I'd guess, having surveyed current gardening sites), positioned in front of the large plate-glass windows that faced busy streets. Three or four blue-suited security guards were also prominently positioned, alert to the revolving doors, and people standing at high desks to fill out forms.

(It was not a bank, by the way, where my father kept as much as a cent. As I play back events in my mind now, I doubt he banked anywhere. My mother found a few envelopes from the IRS in his room after he died, unopened and used as coasters under a bathroom tumbler of scotch; or opened, with the contents discarded. I remember my father bringing any checks he received to the desk of our hotel, where he'd pay our bill, take the remainder in cash, and turn around to tell me, "Let's hit the town, Ace.")

My father found a potted plant that seemed to escape any gaze. He sidled over, stood next to the plant with vigilant nonchalance, fingered a leaf and began to crumble it into his hand. He said he had taken nibs from two or three leaves when he heard heavy feet behind him. Then a slightly bewildered voice:

"Sir, can I . . . what are you . . . *doing*?"

My father ahemmed. "Just . . ." he began, then cleared his throat as he tried to concoct some cunning explanation while he slipped his hand into a pocket, leaves clacking and crumpling. Then my father decided that the best story would also be the truest. He came clean.

"My son," he explained in a tumble. "A pet grasshopper. Got it at camp. We need some green. We're down the street. We didn't know what to do. No grass. We see the palms in the windows, and see ads. Your bank is so friendly. So . . ."

Which the security guard apparently found so preposterous, and so hysterical, that he looked forward to telling the story himself. He shook off my father with a professional glower that threatened to turn into a smile. "Okay," he said. "But get along now. Don't make a habit of it."

My father returned, cackling and triumphant. I'm pretty sure he uncorked a drink, camouflaged in a coffee cup. We sprinkled potted palm crumbles onto Hoppy in his jar.

For the couple of days that Hoppy lasted, I'd sit with his jar in my lap as my father and I watched midday Cubs games. I kept him on my side of the foldout sofa bed my father and I shared (which was never quite folded up), and I would lift his jar to watch Hoppy rub his forelegs, often clutching a potted palm shard.

But of course, life in a glass jar is not healthy for any living being. By the time I was set to return to my mother in the middle of the week, we had found Hoppy utterly still among the litter of palm-leaf crumbles at the bottom of his jar. My mother used a kitchen spoon to dig out a small spot for him to rest in a planter on the fire escape of our apartment.

I have drawn different inferences from Hoppy's story at different times over the years. Hoppy's short life in a glass jar can remind me that love can smother if you're not careful. We should have left Hoppy free to roam on his own for grass, leaves, stems, and flowers, and, for that matter, to fend off the raids of rats and swooping birds. But mostly now, I look back on his story and see an anxious little boy, going back and forth between heartbroken parents, who sought the simple love of a pet.

And I smile all over again to recall my father, crumbling the leaves of a potted palm into his hands to feed a grasshopper his son kept in a glass jar. I think he had begun to sense that I was growing old enough to really see his drinking, and to see through his lies about his drinking, and mad about how it hurt my mother, and made a mess of our lives. But a short-lived and improbable pet of inconsequential size opened something in all of us. Hoppy's abbreviated presence in our fractured family gave my father the chance to get off the floor of life and discover that he could still figure a way to make us laugh and marvel.

A VISION

I sometimes imagine a spacecraft sent to our world from a far-off civilization in which dogs and cats are at the controls. They would begin to draw close, with the blue of the Bering Sea in the spacecraft window. A calico cat is in the pilot's seat, a St. Bernard their copilot, and a poodle navigator just behind them (I know, I know, it sounds like the cast of a *New Yorker* cartoon). Then, in the dark of the spacecraft, a light falls on the science officer, a gray shorthair cat. He's under a headset. Astonishment rises in his eyes. "You gotta see this!" he tells the crew, and flips a live image onto their spacecraft monitor.

They see a human woman as she walks a schnauzer in a park, cooing to the dog, exulting as the little dog leaves a pooh on the grass. Then another image: A man bends down to sprinkle nuggets into a bowl on a floor. A stout white longhair cat waits, swishing their tail with impatience.

"It's . . . it's . . . amazing!" says the science officer. "Apparently, dogs and cats have trained these two-legged creatures to wait on them! Every whim, every need!" he declares.

The other cats and dogs on the crew crowd around the screen in astonishment. "Look!" cries a beagle. "They've even trained the two-legged creatures to pick up their pooh! And celebrate, like they found some rare jewel! How did they ever do that?"

An orange calico on the crew frowns. "I thought the two-legged creatures were cute, but basically untrainable."

"Ahhh but look!" says the science officer. "They've got the two-legged ones waiting on them, on paw and paw! Feeding them! Brushing them! Clipping their toenails! Tending to their most intimate needs! *And thinking that they love it!* They'll treat us like *gods* down there!"

"For Proxima Centauri's sake," the science officer exclaims, "how many crossings of the cosmos did it take to train a whole world of two-legged ones?"

"Billions and billions, I'll bet," says the captain. "But now they've even got the two-legged ones hand-feeding them."

The dogs and cats aboard the spacecraft look on in silent reverence as they hover over the surface of this strange and extraordinary world . . .

NEIL

Neil was not long in our lives. I was about twelve and won him for tossing a Ping-Pong ball into a fishbowl at a holiday event in the basement of a church for which my Auntie Jeri had baked snickerdoodle cookies. I was offered a choice between a small goldfish and a small turtle. I could make no useful eye contact with the goldfish (which is understandable—I had just plinked a Ping-Pong ball over his head). But I drew my finger in front of the gaze of a small turtle, who seemed to lift his little green head and follow my finger. Or perhaps it was simply my wishful thinking.

But Neil Simon, named on the spot, and yes, for the playwright, came home with us in a taxi, nestled on some brightly colored pebbles only a little larger than sugar crystals, at the bottom of the kind of takeout box often used to bring home egg rolls. He spent his first night on that cheery gravel, splashed over the bottom of a tin baking pan in a half inch of water, which was also outfitted by my mother with a small glass bowl with shreds of celery and gnarls of ground beef.

"Steak tartare for Neil!" she declared.

The next day was a Sunday. We found a pet store at which we could purchase a plastic bowl for Neil, with a small, raised island in the center on which he could lounge under a green plastic palm tree, under the sultry sun of my desk lamp.

"Neil the beachcomber!" exclaimed my mother, who in those days worked a couple of shifts a week at Don the Beachcomber's lounge on Rush Street.

We also got a couple of small shakers of flaked turtle food, and a book (pamphlet, really) on how to care for and feed Neil, which suggested that small turtles could live for twenty-five years.

"Ohmygosh," said my mother. "You'll be married. You'll have children who will take care of Neil," a confident assertion I found difficult to credit.

"You'll walk down the aisle with Neil under your arm," predicted my Auntie Chris.

The pamphlet also said that even small turtles liked to swim—it was their nature—and we dipped a turtle toe, if you please, into that advice by pouring about an inch and a half of tepid tap water into the baking pan and holding Neil by the rim of his shell just over the surface. He began to churn his small legs. Then we carefully let him go. He swam! Neil swam! Between our shrieks of delight, we could hear the faintest of small splashes. We were sure we could see a smile on his small green marbled reptilian face.

But then we realized that Neil had no route by which he could leave his tin-sided natatorium when he tired. And so I put my twelve-year-old fingers lightly around the rim of his shell for a lap, and then moved Neil onto the top of a kitchen towel. "Neil! Neil!" we cheered. "Champion!"

Over the next few days, my mother and I bounced ideas off each other that resulted in a plan: Why not fill our bathtub with an inch or so of mild water and let Neil roam the high seas? The slight incline at the back of the tub would offer a place for him to rest between laps, or to crawl up on a dry acrylic beach whenever he chose to signal, "Back to my island, please!"

One afternoon after school, we put down the stopper. We dribbled an inch or so of water in to fill the tub. My mother tested the temperature with her elbow. She nodded, and I took Neil into the palm of my hand and lowered him into the bath-water. Neil swam! In fact, he seemed to frolic! He turned circles! He submerged slightly and then darted up, dolphin-like. He was having fun!

He found the slight incline at the rear of the tub and seemed to want to stay there. We stayed with him for a while, then returned Neil to what we began to call Simon Island.

However, within days, and after a few more splash times, I began to notice a softening in Neil's shell as I cupped him in my hand. My mother sensed this must be due to his diet.

We cut back on the gnarls of ground beef and increased Neil's intake of the flaked food we'd gotten at the pet store. The softening continued—so much so that we decided that to continue his bathtub splash-time could be unhealthy. Neil's ambling across his plastic island slowed. A few times, we nudged him gently to make sure he was still moving, until one day . . . It's still sorrowful to recall.

My mother reminded me, as a good parent should, that Neil had come into our lives as a prize at a church fair. We had no idea how old he was, or how well he had been cared for, and I was a twelve-year-old boy who shouldn't feel that he had done something wrong, or somehow failed Neil and hastened his passing.

"You gave him a lot of fun," my mother assured me. "That's as important as anything."

What our time with Neil reminds me of now is how one of the gifts of pets is the stake we so quickly take in each other's lives. We turn to each other for all kinds of comfort, including— and often maybe mostly—fun.

NO ANIMALS MAY APPLY

I spent a few days as a young reporter in a spiritual community near Kankakee, Illinois, about three weeks before the day their founder assured them that the world would begin to crumble on July 5, 1977, financial systems would collapse, seas would churn, and only their community would be left intact and alive to continue humanity.

"A miscalculation," leaders of the Stelle Group genially informed me when I called a few days after the date of destruction had passed. "We were using the Sumerian calendar," they

explained. "We're recalculating." The next date for world destruction was fixed for twenty-three years later. But in just two or three years the group had dwindled and disbanded, their founder accused of sexual improprieties and bank fraud.

Yet I was surprised by how comfortable I felt during my time among people who had changed their entire existence—sold homes and uprooted their families—to live by the word of a lunatic.

Many had come from backgrounds as teachers, engineers, and executives. Stelle was trying to run their community on water or solar power (kind of necessary, I suppose, for that time they would have to sit alone on the cooling blister of a world). The small school they built had some of the highest test scores in the state (although the classrooms had one-way mirrors for parents to observe their children, like cops looking at perps in an interview room, I thought). They ran a woodworking factory that made quality tables and chairs. The folks I met were friendly and forthcoming. They welcomed me with a Friday night reception that included little quiches, celery and carrot sticks, cheese and crackers, and, even as it was technically against community rules, a little white wine.

"We welcome guests," they explained. "We want you to be comfortable." And when I carefully broached the question, "Should we be here, uh, snacking on quiche and sipping white wine, when, you know, if you folks are right, in a few days, well, you know, the seas will churn and the earth burst into flames?"

"Well, if it is, what can we do?" Their smiles were mild,

resigned, and reassuring. "Why not enjoy tonight and not worry about what we can't control?"

I was not close to signing up, yet I was impressed by their equanimity. Still, over a few days, I had noticed something missing from the confraternity I had seen of snug homes, green lawns, community kitchen and dining hall, and school with a playground and ballyard.

"I haven't seen any dogs," I realized. "Or cats."

Members were ready as I mentioned this.

"We don't include pets in our community," is how they put it. "We find they take time from the time people should spend with each other. They're distracting."

Even then I thought, Well, yes, that's the idea.

Animals demand our time, but they make our hearts swell. They can broaden our view of life by distilling a part of the day down to the basic, mundane, and universal concerns of eat, sleep, scratch, and play that give life to us all. When Noah's world was about to be deluged, he brought animals aboard his ark so those lives we share could go on. And my view of any afterlife worth having includes the company of pets who have been by our sides.

BETTA BING

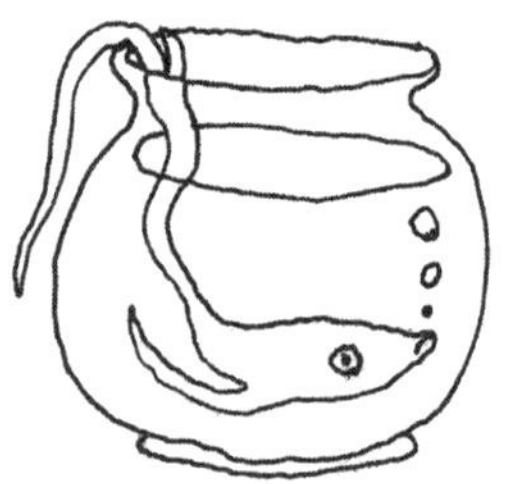

I think we began to bring betta fish into our family when we'd go to the pet store with our older daughter, Elise, in our arms, to buy food and toys for our cat, Leona. We'd see the collection of bright bettas in what looked like full plumage in their see-through plastic bowls on shelves. "See the fish? Look at that one! It's red! Look at that one—it's got a blue tail and red nose!" led naturally to, "Of course we can get one!" The number turned out to be several more.

Elise was so young we didn't have to explain why, say, a greenish betta named Earl was soon succeeded in the bowl by an orangish fish named Jack. We named our first betta after some of my mother's old boyfriends. When she objected, I told her, "Well, we need a large source of names," and when she suggested that I christen the fish with names from some women I knew before I married Caroline, I reminded her that bettas were male fighting fish, and those names wouldn't quite do. We declared a family truce, and awarded our next betta a name of distinction: Salman Fishdie.

We would have five Salman Fishdies. Looking back today, I regret that we provided them mostly with just a clear bowl and sprinkled jots of pet store betta flakes. We would sing to Sami, as we came to call them all, in the kitchen. The radio would be tuned to NPR, for a babble of friendly voices surrounding Sami's glass emporium. And we would hold Elise's small, smiling face over the bowl and on the other side of the glass. But Sami was alone, with an unvaried diet. When other betta-owning families assured us, "Oh, bettas, they don't last long, and the kids just forget about them," we thought we were seeing them through their life span.

Then Elise grew. She was three, then four years old. When a Salman Fishdie left us and I saw him, alas, floating in his bowl next to our coffeemaker in the morning, I would whisk him into a plastic bag, and the bag into my briefcase. We would tell Elise, "Oh, Sami is sick. We're taking him to the doctor," or "Sami is away on vacation. He gets vacations, too. I think he's visiting relatives in Thailand. Say, why don't we have some pad thai tonight?"

I'd stop at a pet shop on the way home from our studios (they began to call me Mr. Betta Man, which I confess I rather liked). I'd walk over to the fish tanks, and there they swam and swam, all over the damned tanks, but the ferocious betta were kept in small round bowls, holding red ones, blue ones, orange ones, yellow bettas with green tails, and blue bettas with white ones, all of them with largish dewy black eyes. A man from the shop would climb onto a stool and try to scoop up the one I thought most favored our most recently departed Salman Fishdie.

"Aww, hell," he told me once. "Just tell your little one that the medicine the doctor gave Sami made him look different," which I tried. Elise was already too smart to entirely believe my solemn explanation. Then again, we both wanted to believe.

I pocketed another Sami one Friday morning and arrived at our NPR studios in a state of despair. A wonderful man named Gary Smith worked the desk then. He would call out "Happy Friday!" to all who passed, with a special smile for me because he knew that our Fridays were our busiest deadline days. He read my despondence immediately. I fished the latest Sami from my briefcase.

"I guess I'll take him into the bathroom . . ." I began to fumble. "You know, down the drain. Burial at sea. Maybe, ah, just in a bin, like a pharaoh or something. But I just can't tell our little girl . . ."

"You can't do that, Scott," Gary told me. "Every living thing has a soul. That little fish has a soul. You and I have to bury him."

Gary clocked out for a break. We walked out into what was then a fringe of greenery next to NPR's front entrance. Buses and taxis rolled by as I leaned down into the soft dirt below a bush and scooped out one handful, then two and three, and finally shook Sami into the opening and covered him up, softly. I stood up, flummoxed about what to say. But Gary's voice was strong.

"Sammy, you were a great little fish," he said, "and a little girl loved you. Thank you." It was as beautiful an evocation of the gift of a life as I've ever heard.

Back home, Caroline gently told me that if a reason for having betta fish in our family was to show our daughter, tenderly, that those we love do not stay around forever, we were squandering such opportunities to make that point, time after time after time.

We brought Elise onto a couch with us. In a kind, warm voice that can only be called motherly, Caroline told our daughter that little Sami had been found floating in his bowl that morning. This meant that he was something she'd probably heard about called *dead*, which meant that he was no longer with us, which was to say that he was no longer alive, breathing, eating, swimming, because he was dead—that word again—and would never come back to life. He was, you know, *dead*.

Elise's small, soft face absorbed the news. I thought I saw an expression cross it as her young heart and mind came to terms with life, love, eternity, and mortality. Then she sat up and raised her arms high to cry out, "Now we can get one in another color!"

Pets are love in our lives. The lessons they hold ahead aren't always the ones we expect.

THE SWEETEST PICTURE IN THE WORLD

The sweetest picture in the world sits on a table in our apartment. A little girl in a pale pink dress, dark-haired and clasping her dark-haired doll under a soft, puffy arm, is leaning forward to lightly press her small, downy-soft head against the soft, fuzzy orange head of a cat.

The little girl is our older daughter, Elise, when she was about two years old and just getting onto her feet. The orange cat is our Leona.

The touch of their heads seems as soft as a kiss. Sunlight brushes their small, precious figures, and makes them glow. Their softness, and their sweetness, is shattering. I imagine the heavens breaking open for the sun to shine on them in that moment, two utterly sweet souls, touching in silence. I wonder: What spark or flash is being sent between them? I think I may almost know.

Leona had walked into our lives after slipping through a cracked-open bathroom window in the apartment of three interns at the British Embassy in Washington, DC. There were Missing Cat announcements up on a few trees. As I walked back from our show one Saturday, I heard a small yelp, saw the face of a small orange cat on a sheet nailed to a tree, and looked down to see that same face by my feet. Before I could reach down, the cat ran off—into an alley, with trucks and delivery vans. I followed to search, crouching and stooping to look under cars, around tires, and the wheels of trash bins, and soon saw a small pair of eyes, looking back.

"That's the little lion," said someone who worked in the garage. "We leave food, but she's shy and scared." They called her Leona—the Lioness.

I went to a deli nearby and brought back a pizza slice, gobbled half, and put the other half out on a plate for Leona. In time, she cautiously peered out from under a dumpster, then advanced on the gooey cheese. "There you go, little one," I told her. "There you go." Within a couple of minutes, she was in my hands, a small orange ball of fur, gnawing nips at my fingers and looking up through wide eyes. I had no cell phone in those days to call the number on the trees, and so I brought Leona home. I had a few bags of treats stored for my former cat, now mourned, and sprinkled them into a soup bowl for Leona. I called the number. The voice of a British Embassy worker, whom I later got to know, informed me that the interns had returned to school in Britain, and new ones had been delayed in their arrival, and I could advance Anglo-American relations by keeping Leona for the weekend.

She was already curled up on a pillow. Her whiskers were at rest. She did not seem eager to return to the teeming streets.

By the time Monday morning arrived, I had begun to sing silly songs to Leona and was hailing her by nicknames (doing a very poor imitation of Johnny Cash warbling out her name as "the Orange Blossom Special"). I had stocked the kitchen with snacks and food. For whatever events transpired in the diplomatic world, by the time I spoke with the embassy official in the early afternoon, she had a different resolution to propose.

"You know, Scott," she said, "I think there must be a reason why this little cat crawled up to you. I have consulted with the highest authorities"—I imagined Her Majesty the Queen herself—"and we all agree. You should keep Leona. But . . ." she added somberly, "you must agree to rear her as a British cat."

No conferences, negotiations, or treaties were necessary. Even when Caroline entered my life soon thereafter (after a few brief verbal skirmishes over the World Cup), Leona was our Little British Pet. We put pictures of David Beckham over her food bowl. I brought her back a Manchester United pennant, purchased while changing planes out of Afghanistan, from a British airport gift shop. When Caroline and I sang out "Breakfast, Little Pet!" to Leona, we imagined (and I often voiced) what I intuited to be her spirited "Righto!"

British friends complained I made Leona sound more like an Australian cat. I think they were being snooty.

Leona soon made herself a part of our lives, as beloved pets do, in a million different ways; an underestimation to be sure. Each of us in our family that soon formed around her felt a spark with Leona.

Caroline and I had become worried over anecdotes from our adoption agency that when children came home, they sometimes showed signs of allergies to pets. We fretted. What would we do if Elise met Leona and began to react allergically? Leona was part of our family, too.

We fell in love with Elise Sylvie Jia Mei Simon the instant she was placed in our arms at the adoption center in Jiangxi, and returned home thirteen time zones east a few days later. Friends waited in our apartment with balloons and champagne. We sat on the sofa with Elise tucked in between us, and the center of adoring attention from her new parents, friends, family, and, we were sure, the world.

Leona hopped onto the sofa. She seemed to crouch slightly and advance carefully toward the little girl who had just been plopped into the midst of her world and was drawing coos and smiles. She took a sniff. Elise seemed to hold up a small hand to her face. We worried that she might be preparing to sneeze at her first whiff of cat dander. Dire possibilities played through our minds and tugged at our hearts. Would we have to give Leona to a friend? Would our beloved Orange Blossom Special have to move on? Wouldn't she be hurt? Wouldn't she be angry? How would we possibly explain to her that it wasn't her fault?

Elise squirmed and fussed a little, then seemed to raise a small-fingered hand to her face again. We took deep, careful breaths—and then our new daughter just beamed at the furry orange living thing right before her, who was of almost the alarmingly same dimensions.

Leona took another sniff. And then *she* sneezed. But luckily for our family, our cat was not allergic to our child.

We had put a crib together for Elise. There was one piece extra. We could never figure out where it was supposed to go, and lived with some fear that when Elise napped or slept she might somehow roll or twist and send herself and the crib crashing. An emergency crew would arrive on the scene and bellow immediately, "Why didn't you put the TU-9 Uni-Conduction Flange in? Didn't you read the instructions?" Thankfully, that never happened.

What thankfully did is that when Elise was put into her crib for a nap, Leona would follow, and station herself right below. At night, she would stay in place below Elise's potentially parlous crib until she sensed Elise had fallen asleep. Only then would she lope back into our company. I have memories to this day of Leona stretched out below Elise's crib, ears almost visibly attuned to any sounds of discomfort or distress above. She would stay there until she heard soft breathing and sensed calm. Our little British cat was on guard, as if Elise were the crown jewels, which she surely was to us. Our family was mother, father, daughter, and cat, and Leona looked out for us all from under that crib.

The spark we see in that photo of toddler and cat putting their heads together may trace back to when we first brought Elise home. Infants from Chinese orphanages, no matter how loving and giving their institutional caregivers, are not held a lot. There are just too many children and not enough caregivers. And the babies do not get much of a chance to crawl. There are simply too many of them in the rows of cribs in an orphanage to put a child down on the floor to explore the world. And many of the floors can be hard and cold.

I got down on my hands and knees on the carpeted floors of our apartment to demonstrate crawling technique to Elise. "You put your right hand down, you put your left knee down . . ." She was not impressed, much less convinced that crawling was a form of transport to be favored. Why crawl in an unfamiliar landscape when willing adults compete to carry you?

But Leona *crawled*. She was a natural, if you please. And so we'd place Elise and Leona on the carpeted floor below the crib, child and cat, where they'd eye one another. Then Leona would take a cautious step or two. "Okay, li'l one," I imagined her saying. "One paw out. Head forward. Other paw out. Legs follow. I been doin' it for years. Got it?" After a few weeks, Elise commenced to squirm, wiggle, and finally, to crawl.

I can't say for certain that Leona knew she was being asked to show Elise how to crawl. But a sincere example is often the most convincing lesson, isn't it? Leona would often crawl carefully over to Elise and place her head against her, that small, downy human Leona had already determined was part of her family in the voyage of life. I imagine some kind of current flashed between them.

In the photo, of course, Elise is on her feet. Inescapably, I remember the small, dear shoes on which she tottered her earliest steps. Leona's small orange head is held softly against Elise's, and her soft orange paws are at rest below, in a burst of sunlight that seems to have found them. What I think I see is a spark between the two, a quiet transmission from one family member to another, our cat to our child, that says, "You made it to your feet, little one. There's lots more ahead."

THIS PHOTO IS PRETTY SWEET, TOO, BUCKAROO

A few years later, our younger daughter perched her most precious pal, a stuffed, hug-worn piggie named Snooks but pronounced "Nukka," in a small dollhouse saddle onto Leona's shoulders (if cats have shoulders). I recall it as a snowy morning, with a pearly sky. Leona seemed to survey the river scene. Paulina crept up to lightly place Nukka around her. He fell off once, twice, and Leona shrugged. But soon Paulina's light touch helped Snooks settle in atop, where he could share Leona's gaze. Just about the most important person in Leona's world had put her most cherished possession around her neck and shoulders, and our little orange cat would carry the load to make her smile.

TOGETHER FOR THE JOURNEY

We humans have been sharing our lives with animals for fifteen thousand years. Anthropological remains suggest that we have grown to regard ourselves as members of the same pack. We look out for each other, forage together, and alert one another to danger. We care for one another with the different and complementary skills of our respective species (dogs have a sharper sense of smell, but no species can open a can of dog food as deftly as a human). We also spring to each other's side to care for, defend, and protect one other. We have learned how to amuse, enrage, and, I don't mind saying, love one another.

There's a famed skeleton of a woman in a tomb, twelve thousand years old, in what is today northern Israel. She was fifty years old at the time of her burial and holds fast to a puppy. They share their grave. Questions race through our minds. Did the woman and the puppy live, and perhaps die, together? Was the woman seeking to protect her puppy from danger? Was she bringing him along to the beyond for their mutual companionship? Or, as the historian Yuval Noah Harari allows himself to speculate, was the puppy placed in the woman's hands in death as an offering to whoever their civilization believed would be standing guard at the admission gates of the hereafter?

Such speculations remind me of Argos.

Argos was the dog of Odysseus, the king of Ithaca, in Homer's *Odyssey.* "There was not a wild beast that could get away from him when he was once on its tracks . . ." Homer wrote in his epic poem. But Odysseus, of course, is away for ten years, at war in Troy. And then away for ten more, losing comrades, as he struggles to return to Ithaca, and to his wife, Penelope, and their son, Telemachus.

Odysseus's Ithaca citizenry, perhaps not unreasonably, assumed him to be dead. A king goes off to war and doesn't return for twenty years—not a parchment or bead message sent back home—and assumptions will be made. But after twenty years, 108 ruthless suitors are in public pursuit of Penelope. They are lined up outside and within Odysseus and Penelope's home like Beyoncé fans before a concert.

Odysseus arrives at his old home in beggar's clothing. He hopes to surprise the legions of beseechers, of whom he has heard. But Argos, who has been left, famished and flea-bitten, on piles of barnyard manure outside their home, is not surprised to see Odysseus at last. He has been waiting with unflagging faith for twenty years. He sees through the beggar's disguise of his master. Argos drops his ears and wags his tail. Odysseus conceals his tears from the assembled, saying only, in Homer's account, "What a noble dog that is on the manure heap."

Homer writes that Odysseus then entered his old residence "and made straight for the riotous pretenders in the hall." But Argos, relieved at the very sight and scent of him, has had his devotion rewarded. His faith has been returned. Argos can be . . . at rest. He takes a last breath and departs this world.

What I have grown to feel over the years is that, until it may be shown otherwise, animals do not share whatever spiritual or scientific understanding we may have developed about death. Therefore, they may not think of death as an end, so much as a door opened to whatever is ahead. I like this faith. I like to think of the puppy and the woman going ahead together. I like to think that Argos believed he was going on to explore whatever new wilds might be ahead for him and Odysseus. They were, after all, partners.

BLESSED BY . . .

We are a family blessed by adoption, in the beings of our two daughters. But I find that my ears tingle a bit when I hear phrases like Adopt-a-Pet. Of course, there is no comparison between bringing children into your life and a dog, cat, or other pet. At the same time, I don't want to turn away from some vital similarities. In each case, we take a precious being into our arms and realize we're responsible. We must give them care, time, and at least good-faith attempts to pass along some lessons in how to grow up to look out for themselves. There will also be previously uncontemplated, and sometimes astounding, duties with which we are entrusted to keep them growing and going.

And there will also be shared moments, emotions, visible tics, and understandings created through daily life and occasional crises that will fix you into each other's lives as family. Most of all, there is the knowledge that adoption is an everlasting commitment. It is for real. It is forever. We don't outgrow, cast off, or get over one another. We are always on each other's sides. We become accomplices, confederates, advocates, cohorts, abettors, movers and shakers, and accessories to each other's lives, for as long as we are here.

When Caroline and I began to try to start a family, in what I'll call nature's traditional and time-honored form, it didn't work. We tried a couple of rounds of fertility treatments, which also did not produce the desired results. We both knew, from our own experience around the world, that there were children who were alone, and needed our love right now. But it was my mother who was bold enough to say, as only a parent might or could, "Look at how much you love Leona. And she's adopted, isn't she?" She knew our love, and used it to pluck exactly the right chord.

Children and animals are different in our lives, but they can be heard on the same wavelength. They both touch us with their innocence, make us laugh with their earnestness, and give us the chance to be useful. They put something priceless in our hands and hearts. Now and then, each of them needs someone, which is us, to take a thorn out of their paw.

PETS IN THE SIEGE OF SARAJEVO

I began to cover the siege of Sarajevo in the summer of 1993, and the most surprising scene on the city's shattered streets was to see someone walking a dog. Parks and streets were raked by sniper fire and shelling, but you could see people waiting on the end of a leash for their dogs to defecate. It was a poignant moment of everyday life in a place that had gone mad.

Every inch of that lively city I grew to love had been scarred. Bullet holes and bomb blasts pitted every brick of every building. You couldn't see through most windows because they had been shattered by bombs, then stuffed with box flaps and rags between the splinters of glass to keep out cold. You couldn't take shelter under trees from blasts or sniper fire, because most of the trees in the parks and along the streets had been chopped down to burn for heat in the kitchen stoves of apartments, while families slept on the floor.

Manoli Wetherell, our recording engineer, and I began to

notice that just about the only people we saw on the streets during long stretches of the day were Sarajevans who had to run between buildings on their way to UN relief supply lines, and people who could not run because they were walking their dogs.

One midmorning we stopped a man walking a full-coated Irish setter across a flat stretch of the park. We walked with him as we spoke, to try to avoid standing still, which could invite the interest of snipers.

"You can't tell a dog, 'There's a war on. Are you crazy? We have to stay inside!'" he told us. "So we listen for lulls in the gunshots and take our chances."

The man had a full beard, gray, which seemed to flutter as we stepped along, like his dog's coat. Full beards came back into fashion during the siege. Smuggling in razor blades was a low priority against food, coffee, socks, and bullets. People used to say that it looked as if the Austro-Hungarian era had returned.

"I have to give him a chance to go outside and do his business," said the man as his setter pulled him away. "And play, too. So do we all, yes? Play outside."

We picked up our pace. There was a woman, smoking as she walked, stepping along with two young girls who jumped up from the grass to hold out their palms so a small, speckled brown-and-white dog could spring up to touch them with his nose. The young girls were ten. The dog, they said, was less than a year old, and had belonged to a six-year-old girl who had lived next door. But one day . . .

Sarajevo abounded in those times with stories that tailed off, unsaid but understood.

"We are without so many friends," one of the girls told us. "This dog is our company. He comes along with us. With us, all the time."

We soon felt, more than heard, a hard whiz of wind across our ears and the top of our heads. Then, a scintilla of a second later, the crack of a rifle shot. Then another. The two girls and the smoking woman, their speckled dog, and Manoli and I flopped onto our hands and knees to scramble across the park, the little dog bouncing at what it took to be play. As I look back on it now, our crumpled forms and a leaping dog could only have made us more conspicuous. But nobody said—nobody thought—"Leave the dog."

We slithered under the eaves of a smashed school building: the girls, the smoker, the dog (named Amina, we learned), me and Manoli, who then took a long drag on a cigarette and delivered what I believe to be the greatest observation I have ever heard while field reporting: "I do not want to get shot," she said, "while doing a fucking pet story."

In the midst of war, and setting aside Manoli's mordant reservation, we began to look for pet stories in the besieged city. We noticed all the unaccompanied cats and dogs left to scrounge over the rubble of streets and buildings. They made it to another day only by the grace of strangers, who would share something from their relief supplies. We met a man with a German shepherd puppy in his arms on a food line. He asked French soldiers from the UN brigade in the city if they could help him get some antidiarrheal pills for his dog.

"My brother and sister, first days of war . . ." he told them. I had a low opinion of the way the United Nations mission upheld its neutrality by essentially helping Serbian units inflict a cruel siege of the city by permitting only a drip of humanitarian supplies to slip through. But something about the little dog in the man's arms, and his appeal for help, pierced the hearts of a few French soldiers. They told him to come back to the line in a couple of days.

We met the man a few days later. He said the soldiers had gotten some of the pills for themselves but gave them to him for his dog. "The soldiers said the doctor say, 'If it should be the pills are for a puppy, break them into powder and have the dog lick them off, two or three fingers, for maybe a week.'" He said his puppy was doing well.

We had grown close to a family with a teenage girl who introduced herself at a security line. Manoli and I became a diversion for her and her friend, on long days on which there was not much to keep them occupied except to grow bored on the floor of a dank basement as they listened for shots and bombs, alert for a possible pause (even snipers take breaks) to try to venture bravely out to bring back relief supplies for their families and neighbors.

Irena Milić was about to turn sixteen. We thought that a girl turning sixteen in such a time and place made a good story. Each day, her family began to tell us more about what happened when the war began one afternoon and they were turned out of their apartment in the Grbavica neighborhood of the city by drunk men with machine guns. It took a few weeks for Irena's mother to tell us, seemingly as casually as she might recount a lunch, how she and her daughter had also been raped that afternoon. "In New York or London," she said, "we would go to a doctor for help, yes? But in the middle of a war here, all we can do is not think about it."

It also took a few weeks for them to tell us about the family parrot they had brought with them across the bridge from Grbavica. They had begun to run low on the bird's food. "And you cannot tell a parrot, 'You must learn to eat something else, my pretty bird,'" said Mrs. Milić. So one day, during a respite from sniper fire, Irena and her mother left the clammy confines of their building's basement and walked a dozen floors to the roof. They had a heartbreaking errand: to shoo away their parrot, urging him to fly across the thin, rusty Drina River that divided the city, in the hope that he would find a family on the other side of the war who would love him.

They sobbed. Their bird, who had lived with them throughout a war, from the first moments in which they all had to roost in a basement, would not fly away from them now. They flapped him off their arms. He flew back. The Milićs then pretended to be mad. He only flapped his way back again. The parrot, confused and uncomprehending, may have finally deduced that their actions sprang from love, and flew to the other side of the war. Mrs. Milić cried so much her daughter told her, "You love that damn bird more than you love me!" Her mother said, "It's close. That's for sure," and they left the roof laughing, crying, and praying for their bird to find safe landing and loving hands.

I borrowed the bird and their family's story and recast it into a novel I would write called *Pretty Birds*. I think I wrote the novel so that I could be certain that in that enclave of my imagination, their parrot would be safe and they would see him again.

One night a Bosnian friend took us to meet a couple, Nadya and Tomislav, who had taken in a dog and a cat they saw on the streets. As Nadya said, "We are sort of a mixed marriage ourselves. He's Orthodox and I'm a Muslim." The front windows of their apartment looked shot out and were boarded over with cardboard flaps, but the couple rocked with laughter.

They had found a dog they now called Aki cowering and full of flies in an empty dumpster. They decided to take him in to be bathed and fed until he could fend for himself on the streets. By the time we met Aki, a year had passed. He was huge, beige, and fluffy from being brushed so much. He had a gift for hearing the high-pitched whine of rocket shells before human ears could detect them. When Aki scrambled under the sofa or a table, Nadya and Tomislav followed.

They had named the small gray cat they found Chula, and said he preferred the powdered milk from French army rations in relief supplies, to American army tinned food. They often had to go to the city's black market to trade one for the other. Chula also liked small French cookies, for which Tomislav had to trade cigarettes.

"But what can I do?" he said. "Tell him I won't? I cannot do that."

We had a fine time—a wonderful time, in fact, with Nadya, Tomislav, our friend Anna, Aki and Chula. Lots of laughter, some sniffles, and coffee. Aki and Chula went from arms to laps, bouncing on us for pets from our hands and hugs from our arms.

"They are so happy with so many people in our place," said Nadya. "They don't know what to do."

Nadya and Tomislav told us that a dog turned up in their apartment block who then gave birth to seven puppies. Five of the little dogs were able to survive because people who had been bombed and shot at in their homes and had the world they had known shattered and shaken over their heads, brought the dogs scraps from their own scarce relief supplies. They took the dogs into their lives.

"The animals," our friend Anna told us, "we are taking care of them because we feel that we need something to live around us. We are feeding the birds, too, because we need them around us. Now more than ever."

I grew to love and admire Sarajevans. When the world turned away from the savagery and murder with which they were assaulted, a city mixed with so many kinds of people who loved to sit over coffee and wine to declaim loudly, late into the night, about art, politics, sports, cinema, and tell racy jokes, they rolled up their sleeves to save themselves. I filed scores of stories on bombings, shootings, and massacres, mass graves, humanitarian missions, and the courage of people called to extraordinary acts. I remember and cherish it all. But I still happily encounter people who tell me, "I remember the pets in Sarajevo." In making room for animals at the lowest times of their lives, Sarajevo showed the world real humanitarian aid.

LOSING THEM

There is a mostly unspoken understanding when we take animals into our lives that we will see them through to their end. We open our hearts to welcome them even as we know that in time, there'll be a hole inside us from losing them a few years hence. The only way around loss is loneliness. That is even harder to bear.

By the midst of her thirteenth year, Leona, our little orange British cat, began to limp. It was devastating to be informed by our vet that there was no pulled muscle or ankle sprain, but cancer in her leg. Yet, they said, the tumors in her leg could be surgically removed, and cats could master their daily rounds with amazing agility thereafter. This turned out to be true. Leona had the operation immediately, and came home puzzled and woozy. In the weeks that followed, our little East Ender seemed largely undeterred. Our hearts melted as Leona leapt, played, and curled up with us. Life went on in our shared rhythms.

But within a few more weeks, Leona was dragging and gnawing at her leg. Cancer had returned. Removing more of Leona's leg seemed cruel, and probably futile if the cancer had continued to grow. Our family had to consider what would be most merciful and wise for Leona, the family member to whom it was hardest to explain such choices as were available, and who would have to bear the costs of any decisions we made.

Other family considerations also tugged. My mother had just died, and then we lost Caroline's father, and then her mother became sick. Our daughters, aged eleven and eight, had to live with a lot of loss in a short space of time. They loved their grandparents, but Leona was a daily part of their lives. Our little orange one, whom Elise and Paulina called Nana, was often part of our daughters' first glimpses of morning. They called her name, they heard the scrambling sound of her paw pads in their bedrooms and felt her soft nose against their chins, her raspy tongue at their fingers, her swirl of a tail tickling their ears. They heard her child-soft mewling throughout the day, which they had learned to read as her cry, *Feed me! Hold me!* Or sometimes, simply, *See me! Over here!*

And of course, Leona curled up with them for their dreams. Would her loss be the one that was too much for them to bear?

As I read these words, I understand, all over again, that the anxieties we're sure we sense in our children are often our own.

The veterinarian told us he had seen some encouraging studies exploring feline cancer treatments at a clinic in Germany. The technology was untested, he said, but if we signed on, Leona might be helped, and help other cats, too. A veterinarian we sought for a second opinion was tenderly skeptical. "I don't want you to waste your money," she told us. I told her, "I don't want to save a little money if it can help save Leona."

We signed on. Leona's treatment went on for weeks. And the cancer advanced.

There wasn't much of a decision to make thereafter. Leona grew sluggish, brittle, exhausted, and was in pain. Caroline and our daughters were soon to depart to visit family. It was decided that before I would fly out to join them, I would be with Leona for her last days. We didn't want our daughters to have to live so close up through another loss. And, as Caroline said, it was also a kind of last promise I owed Leona, as the man who had come upon her in the alley and brought her into our lives.

We tried to keep the night before their departure lighthearted. But at one point Caroline lay down on the floor with our little lioness, her beautiful head next to Leona's, her eyes glistening as she held her against her shoulder. When they left in the morning, our daughters lightly touched Leona's head as she lay on a sofa and said, simply, softly, wistfully, "Bye, Nana."

My appointment with Leona was set for early Monday. And so she and I spent that Sunday watching funny movies, Leona lifted carefully onto my lap. We saw *Tootsie*. We watched *Elf* in the middle of July. Then *My Cousin Vinny*. "The two yoots . . ." Leona would seem to drowse, then be jolted awake by some sharp pain. She didn't want to eat, and she couldn't really sleep.

I sang to her, and laughed for her. I held her in my arms, her head against mine, thinking that the morning couldn't come quick enough to help her, and not wanting it to come at all.

When the hour came, I sang silly, sweet, nonsensical songs to Leona as she slipped away, crooked under one of my arms again, on a table in the vet's office. I remembered the little orange cat who had shown our daughters how to take their first steps and taken up a post in their beds to help see them into sleep. The animals who join us in our lives remind us, time after time and in way after way, that often the best thing we can do for one another in life is just to be there.

The times we see an animal we love into death may make us even more curious about eternity. I mean, if there is such a thing. Will we see the animals with whom we have shared our lives when our own time arrives?

I choose to believe—and I concede that it's a conviction with no logic or science—that there is an afterlife in which I will be reunited with those I have most cherished in my life. This includes my wife, parents, children, family, friends, and my childhood buds, from Avi Cohen to Danny Zemel, and pals like Billy Leavitt and Jim Nayder, who left too soon and got to wherever we're going before me. I choose to believe that I will see, in celestial peace, people I got to love and admire in embattled places, including El Salvador, Ethiopia, Sarajevo, Iraq, and Kosovo. And I wish to believe that all the cats, dogs, hamsters, turtles, and fish we have brought into our lives will be there, too. As I said in the words with which I began this story, we don't make much of a distinction in our family between humans and the other animals. I like to think that love expands our hearts to enfold all we want to hold close.

This is what I choose to believe to get through life. If I'm wrong, I'll try to let you know when the time arrives, though I'm not sure how. In the meantime, I like to imagine Penny, an older cat named Lenore, Leona, and all our Salman Fishdies and other running mates occasionally coming across one another with smiles at some paradisiacal porthole of the hereafter, knowing I'll join them soon. I imagine them joshing one another by asking, "And what silly songs did he sing to you?"

FINDING DAISY, OR THE OTHER WAY AROUND

The idea to bring a dog into our family began months after we'd made our goodbyes to Leona, but we didn't want to do it for a while. There are people who feel such a loss might be assuaged by bringing a new running mate into the family circle as quickly as possible. We felt we had to go through the first five stages of grief, which took the passage of time and tears, before we could reach the point where we'd turn to each other and say, "Hey, want to give it another go?"

Our daughters loved Leona. But they knew her as the orange cat who was attached to their parents when they arrived in our lives. Many of their friends' families had dogs. Our daughters would return to our apartment after an after-school afternoon spent at the home of a pal, and we'd hear how (I'm approximating these names here) Fluffo could jump up and catch a tennis ball, Rufus could play Frisbee, and Bella could dance along to Ke$ha. Our daughters' messaging was unsubtle and effective.

It also, in a way, seemed to confirm that as cats go, Leona was pretty much irreplaceable, at least for a while.

And so we began to explore the possibility of bringing a dog into our lives pretty much the same way people now research what used car or house to buy, or how to replace a water inlet valve in a washing machine. We consulted the World Wide Web.

We researched what certain breeds weighed and ate, and how much they shed. Or shed not. We inquired whether they were friendly to children, or impervious to, or even antagonistic to, their charms. We grew interested in dachshunds. Small enough to easily travel with us, said to be notably intelligent, and winningly affectionate in a family.

We drove into the countryside one Sunday afternoon (which, our family will tell you, I would only do out of my love for them) to visit a dog breeder. She held up endearing dachshund puppies in our smiling faces, but we left without one of them in our arms. We worried that a little dachshund might not be able to make it up and down the stairs, given their spinal construction. And I think we also had some feeling, certainly confirmed by our love for Leona, that somehow, the right pet would find us. After all, she had.

❧ ❧ ❧ ❧

Then Caroline and I were in New York. I was at our studios in Midtown when she called me: "Darling, can you get down to Chelsea?"

I could. I did. Caroline had been walking along the street

after lunch with a friend when she looked into the window of a pet store and saw puppies, yelping and rollicking in shreds of newspaper (more scraps from the *Times* than the *Post*, by the way, at least by the look of the pile). Three young women pressed a small black poodle into Caroline's arms.

"She's the sweetest little dog," they said between sniffles of tears. "But we travel," they explained, "and can't keep her." They were dancers in a local ballet company. "You must get this little dog," they advised Caroline. "You must!"

She held the puppy in her hands, all small feathers of black hair, with a darling, darting pink tongue. The puppy lay back, as if waiting for a spa treatment, and that's when Caroline called to ask me if I could get down to Chelsea. By the time I arrived, the little dog had become conspicuously comfortable in Caroline's arms. Her dark brown eyes shone out of her sable black face, over a small white tuft of a jazzman's goatee. Her eyes seemed to quiver, as if about to burst—unless, of course, we brought her into our lives.

We phoned our daughters. We texted photos. "If we get this little dog, do you promise to walk and feed and take care of her?" "Yes! Yes! Yes!" they promised (a conversation we should have recorded). They even had a name in mind: Daisy.

Caroline and I put our arms around each other and Daisy. We filled out paperwork. And then we learned that to fly her home from New York City, local laws required that she first be neutered. *Ouch.* There would be a forty-eight-hour delay. Our daughters were eager and anxious as they waited. When

I returned in two days, a pet carrier in hand, and rolling my luggage with the other, the man behind the desk at the vet's office where Daisy's procedure had been performed reviewed the paperwork before discharging her.

"Hey, Daisy!" he announced. "You're gonna go to Washington, DC!" And a New York man standing behind me in line sang out—it remains one of my favorite New York stories—"Yeah, Daisy, go take a dump on the president's lawn!"

I returned home to our apartment to a chorus of hugs, kisses, and cooing, all of which, of course, was for Daisy. So far, Daisy has made herself known on the lawns of a few favored embassies and government buildings (we always pick up), but not on the grounds of 1600 Pennsylvania Avenue.

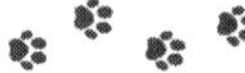

And about Daisy's name:

Caroline and I understood that the decision would rest with our daughters. We wanted them to know that this little poodle who had been brought into our family was *their dog*, after all, and so of course they would cheerfully and devotedly *walk* their dog, *feed* their dog, and care for *their dog* (which has been the case, if only now and again). Insofar as I had thought of a name, I hoped that our French poodle would carry one with some of the élan of France: Colette, Françoise, or Brigitte. I allowed myself to imagine singing out "Bonjour, Colette!" or "Time to *marche*, Brigitte!"

Our daughters chose Daisy from the name of the dog in

R. J. Palacio's novel *Wonder*, which both of our daughters had so loved. I permitted myself some paternal pride that Daisy's name had a literary inspiration, even if I had not read the novel.

A few months after Daisy came into our lives, we saw the film made from *Wonder*. I was moved immensely until about three-quarters of the way into the story, when it became apparent from the tears in the eyes of the stars and the lush sentimental music that the film family's Daisy was not destined to make it to the end of the story. I turned to our daughters in the dark hush of the movie theater and whispered fiercely, "*Why didn't you tell me?* Daisy? Daisy?"

But when I recovered some perspective (the film's heartfelt finish helped), I began to feel that the story of Daisy's name was poignant and wise. Our daughters were children, but they had already seen a lot of loss. Their lives had begun with the loss of their birth parents in China. Then all their grandparents had died in the space of just a few years. Then Leona, our cat. As we grow up, we come to understand that because their time on earth doesn't match our own, the animals we bring into our lives remind us of our frail lifetimes. But this should only put more feeling into our loves and labors, and the care we take with one another.

POO THIS AND POO THAT

Our family can be a little mystified by, and even uneasy about, all the efforts of dog breeders to concoct poodle mixes. People want dogs to have the hypoallergenic fur, vaunted perspicacity, and sage temperament of poodles. So breeders have devised and begotten bernadoodles, shih-poos, labradoodles, schnoodles and cavapoos, pomapoos, sheepadoodles, cockapoos, goldendoodles, yorkipoos, havapoos (a potentially hazardous name, by the way), maltipoos (same), and more. All of them endearing and deserving of love.

Why not just enjoy a poodle?

OBEDIENCE TRAINING— BUT OF WHOM?

Dogs can perform—and be trained to accomplish—many amazing maneuvers. Dogs can be taught to sniff out drugs. They can be trained to herd steers, cows, sheep, goats, and horses, and how to hunt and fetch felled geese, ducks, and grouse. Dogs can be coached to offer salutes with a paw to enchanted humans, to ride skateboards, and to surf. They sit, stay, jump, and retrieve on command at big-name dog shows. Our family has seen dogs in small-town French circuses dance the rhumba. Dogs can be trained to detect, locate, and help dig toward people trapped under tons of rubble. They save lives in scores of ways.

Why, then, can't we teach our dog, Daisy, not to tinkle on our floor when anyone comes to our door?

Daisy bubbled over with the furry froth of puppy charm in our first few months together, all ringlets and licks. We would place a treat for her in the center of the kitchen floor and she would seem to leap on her short legs, then scurry around in a circle, once, twice, three times, in the ecstasy of discovery before concluding, "Wait! That treat! Down on the floor, alone! No barriers! It can be—why shouldn't it be—for me?" and pouncing on the nugget with gratitude and glee. And so, we would do it all over again.

But as she grew, Daisy strained on her leash, leapt into mischief, and was difficult to settle down when we had to give her some kind of puppy medication. We began to feel that some daily disciplines—Sit! Stay! Shake! Snuggle!—might make our time together even more delightful, and safer for Daisy (as well as our sofa, chairs, socks, slacks, closets, and shoes). We gathered recommendations from other families with dogs. They told us how their dogs had graduated from training programs so comprehensive that their dogs could now play the piccolo and were being actively recruited by the Royal Academy of Music.

We finally signed up with an obedience school that dispatched a well-regarded professional dog trainer to our apartment to work with Daisy. And with us. He was bearded, burly, and confident in the way he took Daisy, snugly and happily, into his hands. And he was unblushingly direct about whom he was actually there to train.

"It's you," he said, not making much of an attempt to soften his steely gaze in my direction. "You can teach things to a dog, but if they're not regularly reinforced by those who love them . . ."

We had several sessions in which our trainer would conceal a snack between his fingers and call out "Stay!" or "Sit!" and "Down!" After just a couple of treats, Daisy caught on to the correlation between heeding a call and receiving a snack. All that threatened this smooth process of instruction was my habit of cooing, "Oh, good girl, what a cutie, ooooooooh, did you see her get that snacky-snack?" But Daisy persisted. The instructor moved a couple of sessions to a parking lot, where Daisy soon began to walk beside Caroline with such careful, deliberate choreography they could have been in the procession of a royal wedding.

But Daisy still tinkles on the floor when a visitor comes to our front door. We whisk her briefly out onto the balcony at the first knock or ring, and keep a small towel by our door.

Daisy has trained us in how to respond. I tell visitors that the towel is for me. No one seems to doubt it.

It has also occurred to me over our time together that whenever I pad down our stairs and into our kitchen, Daisy joins along, step for step. She looks up with large, adoring eyes. I prepare coffee. I slide open a drawer and remove a box of matzoh or rye crackers. "Gooood morning, Daze!" I call out softly. "Sooo good to see you!"

Daisy stands below, fixing me with a gaze that says, "You had me at hello."

I reach into the refrigerator for the latest tub of hummus and lift the lid. I break off a piece of cracker. As I dredge a broken edge through the hummus, I catch sight of Daisy's huge, dewy, quivering eyes once more. She seems to tell me, "You are my north, my south, my east, my west."

I take a bite. Crumbs shake down to the kitchen floor, like snow in *Doctor Zhivago*. The emotional moment is so great that Daisy, bless her, has to look down. She slurps the cracker crumbs to conceal the trail of our conspiracy. Assured of the confidentiality of our operation, I proceed to break off another chunk of cracker, haul it through the hummus, take another bite, and shower Daisy in the crispy dust. She looks up now, like a thirsty tulip into the shower of a spring rain.

Daisy is glad I took those obedience lessons. We both know how she has trained me.

It must be noted that Daisy will "stay" in place at that command from our daughters and my wife. But on those few occasions when I have ventured to say "Daisy, stay!" she cocks her head to look at me quizzically, and trots away. I can only conclude that Daisy finds such a direct command from me so incredible that she assumes it to be a mental lapse on my part. She may be right.

STRIPEY: A TWO-PART CONTINUING SAGA

Have I mentioned that our daughters have grown up with a zebra on our balcony? Perhaps I should explain . . .

Caroline and I went on a trip to the Serengeti in the first year of our marriage (tented camps and wine at sunset). I fell in love even more with Caroline, and also took a tumble for zebras. They were in the midst of their annual migration through the Maasai Mara when we saw them, and I was charmed by the way they huddled close together when confronted by predatory, camera-clicking tourists, their chic, wavy black-and-white striping offering camouflage when they banded together in herds. Their striations also reminded me of the vertical railing on our balcony back home. So when our children came into our lives, it seemed only fitting to me that we should fall into company with a zebra.

Here is the essential story I came to tell them:

We were riding the subway one day when our younger daughter saw him: a little zebra standing in front of a man with slick raven hair, a woman in a black jacket who had straight pins in her eyebrows, and a man in a striped shirt and black pants who was wound around the silvery subway pole.

"There's a zebra over there," said Paulina.

Caroline said, "How lovely," but kept her gaze on her book.

"You bet!" I said, as fathers do, and it was finally our oldest, Elise, who said, "Look under the ad for stomach medicine. Shiny black hooves, swishy black tail, a mane like the bristles of a brush."

"My word," said Caroline, softly.

"Told you," said Paulina.

We told the little zebra that we hadn't expected to see him on the subway. He told us he was with his herd on migration when there was a storm and he was separated from his mother.

"So I just kept walking," the zebra said, "and walking. Then I went down through a door that said Elephant & Castle, figuring I'd find some elephants, but I saw only people in a pub. I rode along to Blackhorse Road, but didn't see any horses. I went to Piccadilly Circus, but there was no circus, and I didn't see my mother. I went over to Buttes-Chaumont, but there were no butts I recognized. I kept riding until I got to Zoologischer Garten, because that seemed a good place to look, then Frankfurter Allee, because I was getting a little hungry, but there wasn't much to eat."

"I like grass," the little zebra paused to explain. "Then I took a long ride and swim over to Grand Central at Forty-Second Street, because somebody told me that everybody goes through Grand Central, but I still didn't see my mother. Now I'm here."

Of course we took the little guy home. He didn't blend in

much on the street, but no one seemed surprised. "Great getup!" one man told him. "Do you do birthday parties?" another man asked. One woman came up to the zebra and asked, "What about bat mitzvahs? Do you have a card?"

Elise stepped alongside the zebra and asked, "Do you have a name?" The little zebra just twitched his ears. "What do people—or other zebras—call you?"

"I guess we don't call each other anything," he said. "We live in groups and just know each other. We flatten our ears if we're scared and prick up our ears when we're happy. We hee and haw to make noise. If we see a zebra we're not sure we know, we smell their butt."

Our whole family just went, "Ewwwwwwww!"

"Names are a great invention, aren't they?" Caroline observed.

"What about Stripey?" Paulina suggested, and the little zebra agreed.

"It's easier than butt-sniffing, isn't it?" Elise added.

We took him outside on our balcony, where the rails that keep us from slipping and falling are made of shiny black metal attached to smooth white shafts of concrete. Our daughters noticed something amazing.

"He practically . . . disappears," they said. "You just see his shiny black nose near the top, his black hooves at the bottom, and his twitchy little ears on top."

Stripey ate a whole head of radicchio in two and a half bites. "This is delicious," he told us. "Thank you. Crisp and fresh. What do you have for dessert?"

"How do you know about—?" I asked.

"Your daughters told me on the way here," explained Stripey. "They said, 'Eat lots of lettuce, and they let you have dessert.'" We had an Eli's Chicago cheesecake in the refrigerator.

Two floors above and fifteen apartments over, Mrs. Blanchard sat on her balcony and looked through her field glasses. She kept an eye on the building for everyone, whether they liked it or not. She made sure that everyone had their holiday lights turned off by January 2, even if they were still visiting cousins in Australia and couldn't get back until January 7.

Mrs. Blanchard put down her field glasses and told her husband, "Olivier, the Simons have a zebra on their balcony. He has his snout in a cheesecake."

"That's unlikely, dear," said Mr. Blanchard. He was a teacher and careful to say that unexpected things might be unlikely or improbable, but perhaps not impossible. "Zebras are making their Great Migration across the Serengeti. And they eat grass," Mr. Blanchard added. "Not cheesecake."

"He almost blends in," said Mrs. Blanchard. "But I'm sure I see a zebra."

Mr. Que, the building manager, knocked on our door. "I am told you have a small zebra on your balcony," he began.

"A zebra? On the balcony? Why would we?" I replied, taking care not to tell a whopper. "Why don't you take a look for yourself, Mr. Que?"

Mr. Que paced back and forth, and back and forth, took off his glasses, polished them against his shirt, and put them back on while Stripey held still as a statue. Then Mr. Que shook his head.

"I don't see a zebra. But something funny is going on."

"Tell Mrs. Blanchard we are so grateful for how she looks out for us," Caroline added.

As soon as we heard the door close behind Mr. Que, Stripey let out a long, loud breath and we surrounded him while he gulped air.

"Way to go, Stripey," we told him, and our daughters put their arms around his neck.

"Don't worry," they told Stripey. "We'll take care of you."

Stripey still had a small snail of cheesecake on his nose that Mr. Que had somehow missed.

But what could we do to really help and take care of the zebra who had entered our lives?

"As much fun as it is to have him here, we have to get him back to his herd," said Caroline. "His parents. His friends. The other zebras he depends on, and who depend on him."

"We met Stripey on the subway," Paulina reminded us. "How do we find his herd?"

Stripey burped—and we all laughed.

"I've got a couple of ideas," I said, "about where we can at least find Stripey a few more zebras . . ."

Let me pause Stripey's story here to note: thanks to our family's belief in him, I get zebra ties and pocket squares, zebra mugs, trays, and cards for all family and ceremonial occasions. Stripey is a distinguished and persuasive presence in our lives.

INKY MADE ME THINK

Our family has adjusted our diet to limit food derived from (is that oblique enough?) certain animals. Yet we have made no such effort with seafood. We merrily eat salmon, arctic char, branzini, shrimp, scallops, and all kinds of sushi. And when we're in France—oysters! clams! langoustine! I could go on, and have. And yes, even though our family has kept betta

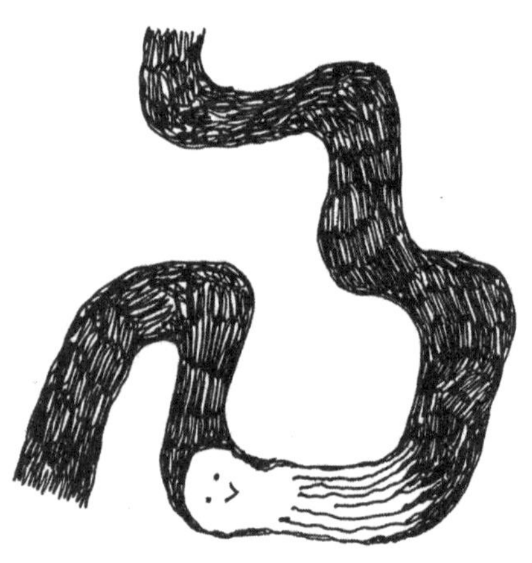

fish as pets, assigned them family names, and written notes to our daughters ostensibly signed by those fish, I assessed fish sentience to be low enough for us to be comfortable about consuming them. Mostly, we still are. Fish, after all, eat fish.

We don't think whales, dolphins, or porpoises should be fished, given their manifest intelligence and empathy. But we are mostly reconciled to accepting the tradition of centuries when it comes to eating seafood. Our species has survived on and feasted on fish for centuries, across all cultures around the world.

Genesis says God made the waters teem with fish for us. Fishermen were considered life-givers. Fish abound in healthy vitamins and nutrients. As a native Midwesterner whose early seafood consumption was mostly breaded fish sticks, there has always been some glamour in seafood for me, too.

For a time, I was especially dazzled by octopus, on those occasions when it was offered, especially grilled and doused with lemon, olive oil, and garlic. When we took a family trip through the Mediterranean, I ordered octopus in all ways it was offered, including whole, all eight legs plopped on top of a pizza at a seaside restaurant.

And then I heard about Inky.

In April 2016, an octopus names Inky, ensconced in a tank at the National Aquarium of New Zealand, apparently noticed a slender gap at the top of his tank and squeezed into and over it like an Olympic pole-vaulter. After landing on a cold stone floor, Inky traversed about eight feet on his suction-cupped limbs and somehow squeezed himself into a drainpipe, down which he slid for about 160 feet, and finally out into Hawke's Bay, on the east coast of New Zealand's North Island.

Think: *Ocean's Octopus*, or *Inky's Great Escape*. His getaway over the top of a tank and down through a long, narrow drainpipe sounds more extraordinary than any heist film.

Rob Yarrell, the national manager of the National Aquarium of New Zealand, told reporters, "I don't think he was unhappy with us, or lonely, as octopus are solitary creatures. But he is such a curious boy. He would want to know what's happening on the outside. That's just his personality."

I began to ask myself: Do I want to eat something—some*one*—with a personality?

Inky had a tank mate, by the way, named Blotchy, who reportedly stayed behind but didn't blab about how his cellie gave the slip to the aquarium.

Blotchy was a cephalopod, but he was no stool pigeon.

It turns out that octopuses are celebrated escape artists. As I learned, there are scores of videos of octopuses, sealed into jars, who figure out how to reach up with their suction-cup limbs to unscrew the lid and make a break from the jar. All I'd be able to do is gurgle.

Octopuses also apparently build shelters on the ocean floor from coconut shells and, for that matter, discarded cans. They look more comfortable than my first couple of bachelor apartments. I marked the words of Alix Harvey, an aquarist at Britain's Marine Biological Association, who told the *New York*

Times that octopuses "have a complex brain, excellent eyesight, and research suggests they have an ability to learn and form mental maps."

I found myself thinking that if I should ever be locked away in a dank, thick-walled prison cell, I'd long to see an Inky show up on visitors' day. Inky would figure out a way over the glass divide between us, and steal back to my cellblock to help plot an escape through the prison's plumbing.

I know I should hesitate to impute human emotions to animals. But I also don't want to close myself off from recognizing impulses, emotions, and feelings we might share with them. We cannot be fellow passengers during our time on earth without developing some of the same concerns about our journeys.

I admire Inky for choosing the risks of freedom over the certainty of security. He made a break from a place in which he was hand-fed, safe, and secure, for the open seas that throng with piranhas, sharks, and risk. After learning about Inky, I couldn't think of a creature—a *someone*—who had the skills to build coconut-shell châteaus on the ocean floor and plot Alcatraz-quality escapes, as winding up on a grill and a plate, doused in lemon and garlic.

Our family continues to eat and enjoy other seafood. So far, I've seen no videos of clams, oysters, or salmon unscrewing the lid of a jar in which they were confined, or building co-op apartments on the ocean floor. But our regard for pets and animals keeps our hearts open. They are there to reach into and teach us.

SECRET OPERATION

One of our daughters is entrusted with a high-security mission. I will be necessarily obscure about details.

There is a big-name lawyer in an office building downtown who brings his family's big, fluffy, friendly mountain breed of a dog with him to the office each day. Except he can't, by building rules. So this esteemed legal advocate tucks his dog into a baby carriage, zips the top closed, and wheels him into his office, under the gaze of security cameras and monitoring guards (who may wonder, "How *old* is that baby by now?").

The dog stays in the lawyer's office suite during the day, no doubt nourishing himself on legal tracts. Our daughter is enlisted to bring the dog out for a walk in the afternoon. This entails lifting and zipping him into the infant carriage, walking him around a green fringe downtown, then folding him into the carriage to be rolled back into the wood-paneled law firm while the dog's esteemed counsel (*owner* doesn't seem to sum up the relationship at all) consults with clients, or argues in courtrooms.

No one says so out loud, but our daughter has the impression that this daily masquerade is well known to all. I think they see that the dog-in-a-baby-carriage routine isn't a scheme or a ruse, but stagecraft. That dog is precious to a family and a father is willing to look a little ridiculous to take care of him. It's love.

WALKING MS. DAISY

Walking our dog Daisy can be both a chore and a hoot, a drudgery and a joy. Walking Daisy in the morning along the river, or at night as we round our block, offers my wife and me opportunities for incidental conversations with neighbors and strangers, even though such schmoozing is typically cut short by Daisy's single-minded search for the urban debris (squashed rats, discarded chicken bones, and "small gifts" left by other dogs) that often eludes the eyes of those of us on two feet.

And of course, there is her unpredictable path to find just the right spot on a patch of lawn to lift a leg and declare, "Daisy was here."

When Daisy encounters people, she is as energetically affable as a car salesman who senses a susceptible customer. She sprints toward them on the end of her leash, as if greeting someone trudging home to the family farmhouse after four years in the trenches at the Western Front.

"You're here!" Daisy seems to say as she rises on her hind

legs and reaches up to the person with her paws. "Right here! I'm amazed! I'm delighted! Let me sniff you! Let me lick you! *I never thought I'd see you!*"

And there are other times, especially when encountering new people who may seem comparatively unmoved by the appearance of our French poodle, I can imagine Daisy responding (it may help to presume a drippy French accent here), "I am *très* cute, eh? You want to pet me, *oui*? I can tell! Don't try to resist! *Je suis irrésistible!*"

And of course, Daisy is usually rewarded, by friends and strangers alike, with pats, snuggles, and "Aren't you *cute*! Aren't you *amazing*! What a *good* dog! What a *great* dog! How *good* it is to see you!"

There is a woman who works the early-morning shift in the office building next to our apartment. Daisy greets this wonderful person as if she'd just spent a year aboard the International Space Station. She rises to wave her paws and settles back down, low to the ground, to signal that she would appreciate a few pats. "Right here! On the back! That's what it's designed for! Ahhh, *mais oui, that's* the spot!"

Daisy's patter seems to change for dogs. She has become fastened into the circle of our family, and to humans. Humans, after all, are her source of support and companionship in all ways. When we walk with Daisy and encounter another dog at the end of a leash held by another human, we two-legged ones may see two four-legged loved ones who belong to the same species. But Daisy often seems to feel that a rival for food and affection has appeared on the horizon. "Bandit at twelve o'clock! Be ready! Paw pad on the trigger!" She sniffs at their nose. Then, if mollified, she trots around to sniff at their backside, including their undersides. "Just gonna sniff now! This won't hurt!"

A neighbor with a male dog for whom Daisy evinced such enthusiasm that we spoke of him as her boyfriend once observed the hindquarters-sniffing and told us, "If she's looking for something in particular, I think she will be disappointed." But Daisy's ardor seemed undimmed.

Daisy recognizes cherished friends from previous walks and barks with a high-pitched elation. We humans at the end of their leashes nod in agreement that we can't, in good conscience, keep our dogs apart, and will trudge through traffic, rain, snow, ice, and furious passersby to bring them together for a shared sniffing. Dogs who are new to Daisy, however, risk a chancier reception.

We have yet to figure out what might provoke Daisy to bark and snap. Sometimes, it seems size matters. She does not want a sturdy German shepherd or a mastiff to think that she finds their dimensions intimidating, so she lifts a lip and emits a growl, and even snaps to so inform them (and then scurries back to safety alongside our feet, and sometimes behind them). The humans with the larger breed rear back on their leashes. All of us hurry to admonish our dogs, "Hey, be good now! Stop that!" Or sometimes, we've become convinced, a dog is so cute, after Daisy's own fashion, that our cooing and compliments, more because of the tones of our voices than our vocabulary of flattery, make Daisy feel that our affections are about to stray. She snarls. We pull back on her leash. Apologies all around.

Monday mornings, Caroline, Daisy, and I aim our walk toward a coffee shop. Caroline waits outside with Daisy while I order coffee drinks at the bar and a slice of banana bread. As I wait inside, I can often spy Daisy through the coffee shop glass. She waits for me to appear in the way that my wife's family in Normandy once waited for the Allies to arrive.

Daisy's eyes grow huge and imploring as I step outside, balancing two drinks and a waxed bag of banana bread. I can see her lick along her snout, preparing for action. Her eyes seem to get close to bursting as I set down the two drinks. "Yes, Daisy, I love you, too," I assure her, and she seems to shiver. "I'm *sooo* glad to see you, too." After I've enjoyed my little joke, perhaps a little too much, the three of us make short work of the banana bread. We laugh and chat and fret and plan, all three of us, and share a meal.

There are often others around us sitting over cups of coffee and slices of something. After Daisy has finished her crumbles of our banana bread, she may trot over to the diners close enough to be reached on her leash. She switches on her conviviality, and the urgent, pleading light in her huge eyes, like a foundling from *Annie* or *Oliver!* "Encore! Encore!" I want to say. "And now, the award for Best Performance of Famishment by a Dog Who Has Just Eaten a Slice of Banana Bread goes to . . ."

But the people in Daisy's target audience are deeply moved.

"What an adorable dog!" they say. "What a charmer! Is she always this friendly?"

"It's your personality," I assure them.

The animals in our lives take us out of ourselves and into the world. Walking Daisy gets us *moving*, in all ways. *Neither snow nor rain nor sleet, heat, nor gloom of night can stay those families with dogs from their appointed walks. Three, four, and sometimes more times a day!*

We run into and pick up conversations with neighbors who might otherwise be just names on the directory, or nods in the elevator. Daisy and the other dogs who reside behind the doors of each hallway in our apartment building open our lives to each other.

"What kind of sweetie is that? Where do they get groomed?" gives way to, "Did you see so-and-so from the fourth floor? He didn't look good. Do you know Marcel, the Frenchie on seven? Your dogs should meet. But Marcel, he dribbles a lot. Have you seen the new dim-sum place on Twenty-Fourth? Did you hear about the so-and-sos? They're in Florida for a couple of weeks. Grandkids. Do you know the so-and-sos on nine? Just back from Mexico. We got a school play coming up. The pumpkins have come in at the grocery store. Did you see Goldie, the setter from the sixth floor? Hobbling a little. Hope she's okay . . ."

Our walks with our animals leave us with the joy of feeling useful. They get us to sniffing, too, for news about our neighbors, our surroundings, and the world around us. We worry when we don't see a neighbor and their companion for a while on our walks. We worry about them both. Part of the way in which animals open our hearts more to the world is the feeling—the fact—that because of them we are blessed with more to love, and more to lose.

And sometimes when we run into Andy, Leader, Sawyer, or another one of Daisy's favorite friends on the end of a leash, I imagine them sniffing each other to say, "Taking them out for a walk, eh? Those humans love that, don't they? Don't let them go back too soon. Walk them around a little. It's good for them . . ."

This testimonial to the enjoyment we take in walking Daisy (except, maybe, when it's pelting rain, or, for that matter, drizzling; or snowing, or sleeting, and each step risks a spill against icy cold concrete; or, come to think of it, when there's cold or wind that can sluice in between the buttons of even a thickly upholstered winter coat; or when we're running late, because Caroline has a Zoom conference coming up, and I have an interview with the interior minister of Moldova; or . . .) is incomplete until I add that Daisy often refuses to let me walk her by myself.

I'll sing out, "Let's go walkin'! Let's go walkin' . . ." pluck up Daisy's leash from where it rests in a coil in our entranceway, and the target of my song often scuttles across the floor and through the side entrance of her travel case. We keep a side of the case opened, outfitted with a faux-fur mat and a changing assortment of stuffed toys, because we feel that Daisy should have a spot in which she can repair to be alone when the clamor of the world grows hard to take, and because when we have zipped her case closed, she scurries off to hide under a bed, where she is even harder to coax out for a walk.

I try more songs. "Daisy dog! You are the cutest little Daisy dog . . ." I scatter treats before her hideout, but she is smart enough to see it's a trap to snatch her from the floor. I offer blandishments. "You are the best girl! You are the greatest little dog since Lassie!" I promise that we will stop for yogurt on our amble. I tell her, "I am sooo lucky to be able to walk with you!" But Daisy stays in her lair, resolutely. I have no choice but to accept hers. I stretch out a couple of paper mats should she feel the need when I am away. I'll miss the coffee I would have gotten when I got Daisy her yogurt. But when you're running mates, you win, lose, or walk together.

FRENCH POODLE HOCKEY

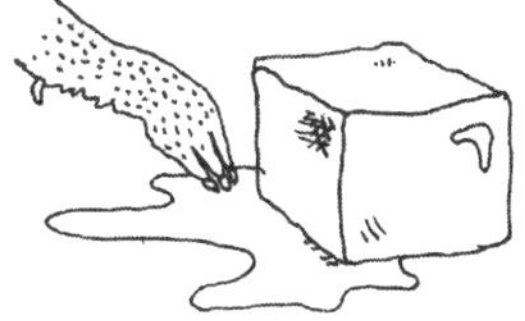

One day, one of us let slip an ice cube from our hands onto the kitchen floor. Daisy scurried over to sniff and lick it. Then she began to bat it with a paw, and saw it zip across the slick floor. She batted it again. Then again. And then again, against the baseboard of the wall, and it bounced back. Goal, Daisy!

We began to drop ice cubes onto the floor for Daisy's entertainment. *Gooo, Daisy! Goooooal, Daisy Richard Simone!* Or was it for our own entertainment? I began to do poodle hockey play-by-play, in an excruciating, ostensibly French Canadian accent. "Daisy has zee puck! She skates toward zee goal! *Magnifique*, Daisy!"

The season went on for perhaps a year. But then, as Daisy grew into her teenage dog years, she seemed to lose interest, as teens will. She grew out of the game even as I didn't.

Just the other morning, on an urge, I broke off an ice chip and placed it on the kitchen floor in front of Daisy's food bowl.

Daisy seemed to examine the ice chip, then looked up at me. She gave it one desultory bat, then another, and then seemed to figure she had done quite enough for old times' sake. She looked up at me. Her gaze seemed to say, "Deserves a treat now, don't you think?"

ULYSSES S. CAT

Ulysses was my mother's cat. Welcomed late in her life, he was a chunky orange Scottish Fold with endearing floppy ears and a broad, flat face that looked, as either my mother or I put it, as if he had been running full steam after a mouse when a door opened and . . . *splat!*

Uly, as we came to call Ulysses, would lower his furry face into his bowl and learn, time and again, that his mouth was set so far back he had to mash his pink nose down against the bottom to reach his food. Then he'd raise his head, after chomping and licking to short-lived satisfaction, and shake his hefty whiskers.

Crumbs would fall like coal ash in old Scotland from Ulysses's tangerine countenance. His small, squashed face gave him the winsome frown of a fussy infant.

Uly was not named from Joyce's novel or Homer's poem, but for Ulysses S. Grant, the son of Illinois who had been the great Civil War general to whom Lincoln wanted to scnd a case of whiskey, and the better-than-is-generally-credited eighteenth president of the United States. His name was engineered to endear him to my stepfather, Ralph Newman, who ran the Abraham Lincoln Bookshop in Chicago and helped found the Civil War Round Table. But no such strategy turned out to be necessary.

Uly came into my mother and Ralph's life not long before Ralph's health began to decline. Ralph had heart problems, and so a hospital bed was moved into his home office, with a wheelchair alongside for his increasingly brief forays into the city he loved.

Uly was almost always curled up with Ralph when I came to visit. He would sit on Ralph's lap as Ralph sat in his wheelchair and we discussed the Cubs, the Bulls, or local politics. When Ralph would slip into his bed, often by the middle of the afternoon, Uly would bound up to take his station by Ralph's middle, settled among sheets, a blanket, and spare pillows, a half-empty tray of tea and toast nearby. But Uly would ignore the crumbs and just curl up by Ralph. Ralph often closed his eyes as he—as they—listened to music. A favorite, and certainly the song I hear in my mind as I think of them together, with my mother looking in from the doorway and smiling softly, was Louis Armstrong singing "I see trees of green / Red roses too . . ."

I know from our conversations that Ralph took to his sick-bed with regrets. "I wish I could do more for your mother," he'd say. "I mean, look at the way she's looked after me. I wish I hadn't had some of my . . . problems." He'd mention a few other names and situations. "But there's not much I can do about any of that now," he'd go on. "I'm here."

I'd tell Ralph how we loved him, and that none of what caused him dismay was worth holding in his heart other than that love. His eyes would often begin to close. His breathing would slow. And Ulysses would draw in even closer, under Ralph's arm. He kept vigil for our family, asking of Ralph only to be held close. At what he knew to be the end of his days, Ralph also could know—could feel—that he was what Uly looked forward to in his life. When Ralph left us, Uly prowled the apartment, mewling, his scowl sadder than ever as he searched the halls for his pal, his sidekick, the big, soft, warm-armed rock in his life.

In the times that followed Ralph's passing, Ulysses turned his affections and attentions completely over to my mother. My mother returned them in full. And more. She cooed to Ulysses, combed him, stroked him, sang to him. "Mommy looo-ves her little Ulysses. Mother looo-ves her fur-ree little boy . . ."

"Your little brother," she would tell me with a wily grin between choruses. "Uly, say hello to your big brother."

My furry orange brother was civil to me on visits, but he would snap at our daughters, then a toddler and an infant, when they reached out their small hands to touch him. This alarmed and confounded them—and Caroline and me. Leona, our own cat at home, adored them and lived for their hands to touch, pet, tickle, and scratch her tummy and back. She was also orange, albeit easily half the size of Ulysses.

No doubt we dismissed Uly with some epithets at the time for snapping at our daughters. But what I see now is that while Ulysses was willing to share the attentions of my mother with her friends and, say, me and my wife, and, for that matter, Matthew, the man who would become her last husband, our children seemed to poach on what he took to be a special feature of his world. When my mother saw our daughters, she cooed to them, hugged, stroked, and kissed them, in the voice Uly thought she saved to speak to him only.

This made Uly jealous—and anxious. His heart had already been broken when Ralph disappeared from his life. And now he must have feared that he had somehow lost my mother's affections, too.

Ulysses would die a few years later (it turns out that the small, squashed face and beguiling folded ears of his breed can indicate cartilage weakness). We encouraged my mother to, in time, bring another cat into her life. We offered to help but she declined, and reminded us, politely but pointedly, that any pet we brought into her life in her eighties would likely outlive her.

"And I can't do that to a little cat," she would say. "My heart would break just to think of them wandering around and wondering, 'What happened? Did I do something wrong?'"

Time and life can revise how we hold those we've known in our memories. When we remember Uly now, it's for the warmth he found at Ralph's side. When my stepfather felt sick, frail, and useless, Ulysses S. Cat assured him that comfort and charm could still be found in his companionship. Uly's joy, and even his jealous snaps, seem endearing to us now.

THE GULLS, THE GULLS

Our family is blessed to spend several weeks every year in coastal Normandy, a region of France known for its remarkable history, dazzling art, artful cuisine, and the clamor of seagulls.

Seagulls can caw like crows, clack like castanets, cackle like witches, jeer like teens, and whine and whimper in a way that grabs your heart. Alas, their extraordinary, cacophonous performance customarily occurs during the evening hours, when even exuberant French people are turning in for a restorative sleep. We know. Pardon my yawn . . .

Normandy's seagulls are nobody's pets. In a sense, we are theirs. Seagulls are a protected population in parts of coastal Normandy, and let's just say it sometimes seems as if they run our seaside town. When you walk to a bakery in the morning, they are already along sidewalks, feasting over the earlier breakfast of leftovers and discards they have pecked out of plastic trash bags. You can watch them crunching, with practiced delicacy, on bits and pieces of discarded *crevettes, jambon, crêpes,* and *haricots verts.*

I remember one seagull in particular from a few years ago who used to greet us in the morning. He had a rolling, imperious strut and a commanding squawk, and so we used to call him the Mayor. This got shortened to "Rahm," for the man who was then the mayor of Chicago. Rahm the Seagull would lift his webbed feet and hasten his swaggering step when someone, including us, left the bakeshop with a baguette nosing out from its bag.

"Dat's a great *effing* baguette ya got dere!" we imagined Rahm calling out. "Great *effing* baguette. Ya gonna eat that effer all by yerself?"

We looked forward to his official visits on our street, though I suspect by now he has been succeeded in high office.

There is usually a family of gulls on the roof just across from our apartment windows by the time we arrive in the early summer: two parents and the two or three little winged fuzzball chicks. They have made nests in gutters and under eaves. We see the gull parents swoop in across the roof and waddle over to their chicks with worms, leaves, or *frites,* spilled on the street, in their mouths. The parents lean over their chicks, who open their small beaks, wide and pink, to receive their delivery. No signature required. Thanks for your business!

We watch this delivery several times a day, and cheer. "Okay, little one, get that fish! Open wide for that bread crust!" And after a few weeks, we begin to see the parents nudge them gently (or not so gently) from the nest to fly off and make their own way in the world. And begin their own families. All this takes place on a roof next door, just outside our windows, where animals we have grown to love show us whole life passages, birth to adolescence to maturity, spent over just the few weeks of a summer.

One night, Caroline and I were having dinner just off the town square, our daughters choosing to slurp noodles at home, when a couple at the table next to us paid their check and departed in the late light of a Normandy summer night. We nodded. And then, while we perused cheeses, a seagull made herself comfortable at their vacated table. The gull pecked at some bread, then seemed to sort through the folds of a napkin, looking for something more; perhaps the aroma of a Normandy *homard* still clung to it.

The proprietor came out to the sidewalk flapping his arms more than the seagull, who finished her snack at an unhurried pace, undisturbed by the yapping and gyrations of another member of the two-legged species with whom the gulls were kind enough to share their province.

"What can you do?" the proprietor explained. "Nothing. *Nothing.* The birds are protected here. They do what they want."

The proprietor returned inside to attend to two-legged diners with credit cards. Our winged and web-footed neighbor finished her repast, seemed to offer a prim belch, and plopped down to the street for a postprandial stroll down the white stripe in the middle of the road. I thought I could discern a slight grin on her beak. She might have been musing, "Normandy, *mon ami.* Seagulls run it."

The seagulls do raise a terrific clatter at night all through town. They seem to call out to one another and to caw at the moon, the clouds, and the stars. Science has found that in this cacophony, there are calls for romance, for baby chicks to find their way back, and warnings that birds of prey may lie in wait on branches and roofs nearby. I like to think I can hear, in their squawks and screeches, alerts like, "Three streets down from the beach, second building over, green garbage bin rolled out to the street. Top popped and open to scavenging! Bits of pain au chocolat! Mille-feuilles! Madeleines! See you there!"

I am, after all, a city kid. I find it reassuring, if not always restful, to hear the noises all around us of life at night that the gulls bring.

CAMPAIGNING FOR CAT

Our younger daughter, Paulina, loves Daisy but assiduously campaigned for us to bring a cat into our family. I think she found a commonality in the inscrutable cool of cats.

Caroline and I also love cats. But, as parents do, we played for time by citing dozens of practical reservations. We travel with Daisy. How would we fly with both Daisy and a cat in tow and under adjoining seats? Or if we left our cat behind, how would they be cared for, and by whom? And if we brought a cat into our lives now, who would feed them and change their litter box? We had received all kinds of emphatic and moving assurances from our daughters before bringing Daisy aboard, that they would feed her, walk her, groom her, cherish her, and look out for her every whim. Those fervent promises soon fell away, making Caroline Daisy's supreme provider.

And even if our daughters joined in care for a cat, to whom would those duties fall after our daughters departed our apartment for college and work? Etc.

Aren't you convinced?

Paulina was not. And so after cold logic proved unavailing, I deployed political doublespeak. You don't interview as many politicians as I have without picking up a few pointers on nonsensical rhetoric. When Paulina said, "I want a cat!" I'd reply, "Yes you do! I understand that. You want a cat! I hear you! I respect that! And I think we should have that conversation!" Paulina might repeat, "Okay then, I think we should get a cat." I'd come back with, "Yes, that's a conversation we absolutely should have! I'm glad you raised the question. We should have that conversation, shouldn't we? Thank you for raising it."

Next, Paulina's gaze would narrow and her voice would flatten.

"Well, we're having that conversation right now," she'd say. "And you can end it by saying yes."

Then the universe began to conspire. Cat cafés, places in which you were invited to have a cup of tepid coffee while being nosed and crawled over by adorable cats in need of families, seemed to multiply on the streets along our daily routes. We'd press our noses against the glass, but hurry along. Then we found ourselves in Paris one night across from a restaurant in which cats were essentially part of the staff, curled up on the backs of couches and making themselves comfortable on bench seating. Of course we had dinner there. Both our daughters (and, to confess, even Caroline and I) had to enthuse, "Awww, look at that one! Look at that one, too! How cute!" I forget what we ate, but I remember the feline personnel.

Then that summer we went inside a small, centuries-old church in a Normandy town near ours. It was dark inside but moving, with the old painting and statuary lit by the flickering of devotional candles. We stopped to light candles in front of an altar to a nun, St. Thérèse of Lisieux. When we slipped back outside into daylight on the square, Paulina informed us, "I prayed for a cat."

Caroline reminded us that the purpose of prayer isn't to send a wish list of desires soaring upward. It is to focus our hearts and minds on love and service. She was utterly correct and convincing. But it soon became hard to believe that saints hadn't heard Paulina Simon's call for heavenly intercession. Unaccompanied cats began to appear before us. We began to see lone cats scurry across streets and take cover under parked cars. Our eyes often locked with theirs, which sent shivers through our hearts. Were we being called to take them in? And yet, they looked well fed and lovingly cared for. We didn't want to whisk off someone's cat who was already in a family and simply accustomed to roaming freely in their surroundings.

One cat in particular in town seemed to cross our path. He was gray, groomed, and fluffy, and we'd often see him on the street in the morning, and on our return from restaurants or movies in the evening, when his eyes would seem to glow. We didn't see the little cat scratching at trash cans for food, or roaming about to look for a familiar door. He looked healthy and at home, so we left him there, whoever he was, on the assumption that the cat was our neighbor, fitting happily into a family that felt it was safe for him to ramble on the street. Yet when it came time for us to leave that summer, the cat was still in our thoughts. We began to look at the websites of organizations that offered the chance to take in foster cats until families can be found for them.

And then, with almost biblical significance, our friends Maggie and Erick had a flood. This is a rare misfortune to suffer when you live on the upper floor of an apartment building, but Maggie and Erick are rare people. Some plumbing burst in a wall, and the waters rose. They escaped with a few personal items, their rescue dog, Ziva, and their cat, whom they call Cat. They moved into a hotel nearby while insurance adjusters contended, and repair work proceeded and stalled.

Two people, a dog, and a cat in a small hotel room.

Cat had a career in diplomacy. He was a rescue cat who had been brought into their lives to help settle down their rescue dog. But the small hotel room aggravated his ordinarily ambassadorial instincts. He clawed at the unfamiliar bedding and furniture with which he was suddenly surrounded, to make himself more at home. This left the bed and sofa appearing as if a pack of leopards had ransacked the room. The young couple had heard that our family might be interested in welcoming a cat who was in recovery from the loss of his home. Paulina did not even need to remind us of our vow.

We draped sheets, tablecloths, blankets, and plastic wrapping over our recliner, reading chair, and sofas, and opened our door to Cat, whom we also began to call Gato Blanco. He is huge, fluffy, and seems to fling clumps of white fur from his girth as he prowls with majesty over our floors, tables, and, for that matter, our heads and laps.

Huge, by the way, is too slight a description of Gato. I do not want to fluff-shame this cat we cherish, but I also do not want to diminish the impression he makes. Gato is Hitchcockian. Old Depression-era cartoons of fat cats under top hats, smoking cigars? They look like Gato. But he is the Orson Welles, the King Henry VIII, of cats, handsomely rotund, imperious, sage, and unflappable. And Paulina really does look after him. We decided to take in a cat—and got a cat and then some.

IN SYNC

There's a soft pink nose on my nose, two dark eyes beaming into mine, and a touch of breath across my chest. *Not now,* I murmur. *It's 3:15 in the morning. I must be up at 4:30.* Then, a sack of cement thumps on my chest. It settles in—makes itself comfortable. *Gato.*

"I . . . have to . . ." I try to eke out enough breath from my chest to croak, "sleep . . . a little more . . ."

Gato shuts his eyes and lowers his great white head onto his paws. I modify my breathing and close my eyes, too. Soon we are alternating our snorts and wheezes like bleats and growls in a jazz improv. Synchronized snoring . . .

DELICATE DIPLOMACY

Daisy, of course, did not have a vote when it came to bringing Gato Blanco aboard our family as a foster cat. She loves people, but she does not love sharing attention. And of course, we felt that we had to make Gato feel welcome. And so there was (still is) a lot of cooing, cuddling, and treats. Daisy seemed almost reconciled at first, perhaps out of an assumption that Gato was a visitor who would be received and fussed over, and soon depart, after the exchange of a few air kisses.

But then the hours became days, and then weeks, and then the months rose to more than a year, and Gato, our foster cat, had become fixed into our family. Harrrumph . . .

Daisy and Gato did not frolic or nap together. Daisy would occasionally swerve to yap at Gato. Or Gato would raise a claw and swipe at Daisy (he had the weight advantage, after all). I wondered if we ought to station surveillance cameras in strategic spots, to deduce whom best to scold. Most of the time we just invoked an all-embracing "Hey, can't we all just get along?"

And between rivalries and eruptions, Daisy made thought-ful accommodations for the cat she considered to be, after all, some kind of illicit squatter in her environs. She permitted Gato to snooze in her dog bed when it was otherwise empty. She ceded to Gato a spot on a rolled-up rug from Afghanistan that was under our pool table. And she accepted Gato curling up in a corner of Paulina's bed, to look out for her at night. It was as if (I know I may be thinking wishfully here) cat and dog had divided up sentry duties.

But Daisy has refused to concede so much as a scintilla of closeness to Caroline. She curls up by her at night, and woofs and howls if Gato sets so much as a paw within what she takes to be her sphere of influence next to Caroline. There is an occa-sional commotion in the middle of the night, but the truce lines Daisy has laid down seem to hold. Gato's diplomatic training persisted. Cat and dog have figured a way to go on together. I am impressed, despite occasional border intrusions, by their armistice.

THE JOY OF BABBLE

After quite a few years of working with words, I've come to feel that some of the closeness we have to the animals in our lives is because our words are essentially useless with them. Dogs might come to recognize commands like "Sit" or "Stay," or a pronouncement like "Bad dog!" delivered over a demolished dessert discovered on a kitchen floor. But that's a limited vocabulary. It may have as much to do with the tone of our voices and various signals we send with our hands and fingers. Ask your dog, "Did you see the balance of trade stats? What's the deal with this Bitcoin stuff?" "Is Adam Sandler an underrated dramatic actor?" "Did you see that story in the *Times* today? Outrageous! Can I leave it by your food bowl?" and they'll probably be unmoved (though Daisy, of course, insists that we leave *Le Monde* by her bowl).

The fact that most of our words are heard by the animals in our lives as mere sounds, unintelligible and unmusical, is often lost on us. Or rather, I think that we know, but choose to ignore that fact and continue to blather at them. "Goood morning, *ma chère* Daisy! Goood morning, our noble Gato Blanco! Goood evening, our dear Bagel! Tell me, Gato: Did you like the chicken nibble treats more than the liver flavor? Bagel: How goes the wheel? Daisy: Would you like to take a walk down Twenty-Fifth and stop in at that new deli? Do I hear a yes?"

I think that's because we not only hear ourselves, but begin to intuit their voices, too. We infer replies from our animals that are distilled in our own imaginations and hearts, informed by the feelings we have for our running mates. This is empathy, and it goes back and forth. Our animals can sense those times we are lonely, sad, scared, or hurt, and they draw near, and often curl up by our side, knowing their closeness and warmth is the most direct and compelling comfort there can be. And we begin to understand that our welcoming hands and laps, and even the sound of our babble, let them know we are part of the same living enterprise.

Matthew, my mother's third and final husband, had no experience with household pets when he met my mother. He wondered how it was that she could keep up a constant chatter with Ulysses. "Does my boy want a snack?" she'd ask. "Is our boy hungry? Would our boy like to watch *The Sopranos*?"

"He doesn't understand any of that, you know," he would point out. "I mean, knock yourself out, but it's all lost on him."

Yet in time, as he began to know my mother, he began to care about Ulysses, too. He grew to appreciate how a cat's side of the conversation could be wordless but resonant. Words are not required to speak heart-to-heart, so much as tone and touch.

THE CHIMES WE HEAR IN OUR HEART

Daisy brims over with excitement to hear a knock or ring at our door (I always think of the Sondheim lyric: "Phone rings, door chimes, in comes company!"), whether the visitor is a friend, family member, or a neighbor with a misdirected piece of mail. Sometimes all we can do is hold Daisy in our arms as she quivers with anticipation.

Daisy has no guile, slyness, or subterfuge. She gets excited, she gets hungry, and she announces it to the world. We admire that. She does not act, pretend, connive, or flatter to gain what she needs and desires. Daisy expresses herself instantly, directly, and point-blank, by barks, growls, romps, snuggles, snarls, and pees. She is open, vulnerable, and needy, as all of us animals are who crave and require company, associations, relationships, and others to laugh or groan along with or at our hijinks.

And when you take an animal into your life, both lives

begin to revolve around and accommodate each other's appetites, sleep schedules, loves, and all our most intimate daily details. The exchange may not be equal, but it does run both ways.

Sometimes we may regret that our animals cannot understand our words. "Not now!" we may snap at them. Or "Hold still!" "Come back!" "What happened?" and queries like, "Where did I put the remote?" and "What did you just swallow?" and "You remember Aunt Claire, don't you?" But because we lack that spoken language, we can talk to our animals without being questioned, contradicted, or misunderstood. It is a love that grows as we are each at a loss for words.

SCHOOL DAZE

Daisy has decided to go to school with our daughters. She clambers into the car, sits on one of their laps, and holds her head high in expectation. French test today? *Je suis prête!* Math? If y(x–1) = z, then x . . .

They pull into school, a daughter opens the passenger door, and soon Daisy stands on her back legs, reaching up for coos, kisses, and cuddles from parochial schoolgirls in plaid skirts. "Hellooo, Daisy! How are you, sweet girl! You are sooo cute, Daisy!"

If I'm in the car, too, one of the young women might say—might—"Oh, Mr. Simon. Hi to you, too." I am reconciled to that.

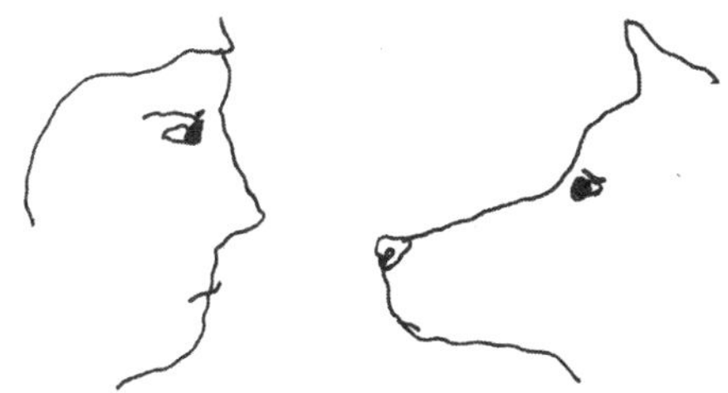

MISS ANITA WOULD NOT LEAVE

"Hi there, Simon family. There's a hurricane bearing down on this area. We have a vehicle here to take you and your family to safety. But you'll have to leave your pets. You know, that ashy-gray dog with huge brown eyes in your arms. And that cat on your shoulder—looks like a cloud with eyes and a tail. And the—what's that little guy in the cage? Oh yeah, hamster. Well, say goodbye. We gotta leave now. Ready?"

What would you do?

I'm glad our family has never had to contend with the question. And if it were to be put to a family vote on the spot, I have little doubt of the result.

Actually, I'm pretty sure I'd raise my hand to say, "I'll stay." And then try to dissuade the rest of our family from doing the same.

I was in Mississippi and then Louisiana during the weeks after Hurricane Katrina struck in 2005, with producer Peter Breslow and our recording engineer, Josh Rogosin (who would go on to so beautifully record NPR's esteemed *Tiny Desk Concerts*). We saw people sleeping on roofs with dogs and cats in their arms, and encountered people who slipped back over police barricades as soon as the waters receded, to rush back for the pets they had left to fend for themselves in their family homes. Many, we began to hear, had come back to make heart-wrenching discoveries.

Pets were not included under evacuation orders, or accommodated in emergency shelters. You can appreciate the original wisdom of this rule. Space is limited in boats, buses, and other emergency vehicles. You don't want to leave behind, say, somebody's uncle in order to make room in a boat for a cocker spaniel. And emergency shelters, in which I've spent a fair amount of time, are often chaotic and congested. The volunteers and medical staff are already overburdened without having to provide space, food, and care for frightened cats and dogs, howling, mewling, and hungry.

And yet, pets are part of our families and communities. As many as a third of those people who refuse to leave their homes in emergencies, we learned in later investigations, choose to stay through danger and destruction because they don't want to abandon their pets to the peril just ahead.

I don't compare the loss of 1,139 human beings who were killed during Hurricane Katrina to those of an estimated 150,000 dogs, cats, and other animals who died in the storm. But you can't be unmoved by the scale of that loss. Those animals were part of their family's lives, and constant companions to those on their own. We didn't meet a single Mississippian or

Louisianan who had left behind a pet who wasn't anxious and regretful about leaving them. It was often the loss they feared most, and found most irreplaceable.

We went to a funeral one afternoon after Katrina. Emma Anita Wagner Seals was eighty-one. She had grown up in Wiesbaden, in what was then West Germany, and left to marry a US Air Force man, Jimmy Seals, stationed at an air base nearby.

"But she cursed like a sailor," folks at her graveside remembered. There were about twenty-five of us, under a tin roof in a veterans' cemetery in Biloxi. "Miss Anita was a force of nature," many said, which was an extraordinary tribute coming from folks who had just seen the forces of nature, close up and furious, in recent days.

Rain splashed on the light tin roof, each ping ominous after the storm. But a minister said, "The grounds you see here have been ravaged by Katrina. But it will be green again. It will be pretty again."

We learned that Emma Anita Wagner and Jimmy Seals spent most of his deployment in Germany, moved through various air bases in the United States, and eventually settled in Pass Christian, Mississippi. They never had children. They took in stray animals and made them their family—dogs, cats, even a neighborhood raccoon, whom they put up in their garage. Jimmy Seals had died about eleven years before, and Miss Anita, as they called her in town, grew close to the fire and paramedic crews who took to looking in on her. She cooked for them, joked with them, and shared the companionship of her animals with these young people in stressful jobs, spending shifts away from their families.

"She was there to take care of all of us," said a woman on an ambulance crew. No one knew exactly how many animals were at home with her when they came to check on Miss Anita as they urged residents to leave town before Katrina rolled ashore.

"But we knew Miss Anita wouldn't leave," said a paramedic. *"Couldn't."*

"All of her animals," added another. "She couldn't leave them." The crew began to recall: two or three dogs, one, two, three, four cats. "Who knows?" they kept saying. "Animals were her life. All around her. Always."

I tried hard not to think about, and then could not help but imagine, Miss Anita, Emma Anita Wagner Seals, in her home when the storm hit. She would have been surrounded by, and probably holding onto, the animals who were her life, as the winds of the storm must have smashed windows and whipped apart walls, and the frothing, angry seawaters crashed around them.

They could not be safe. They would not be spared. But they could be together.

And in 2006, the US Congress changed the law. Emergency services must now include household pets and service animals when they order people to leave an area in the face of disaster. Even a deeply divided Congress could see the need to keep families together.

IT'S A BIRD, IT'S A PLANE, IT'S . . .

It's winter, and my wife Caroline slides open the balcony door slightly to salute and nourish the denizens of our worm bin. Daisy comes out to announce her presence to dogs and their people across the way. Gato Blanco squeezes his own ample presence through the door, too. I look up for a moment to glimpse the happy scene. Caroline comes back inside from the cold, motioning in Daisy with her hands and most soothing voice.

Then she sees, or rather does not see, Gato.

He is not scrunched under a balcony chair, or against the worm bin. I scurry around inside; he has not slipped back into the apartment, either, to hop back onto a warm chair or atop the table he has claimed as his province, or to take up a position among shoes, umbrellas, and brown boxes in a closet.

Where is Gato? Could he have leapt all the way up into one of the planter boxes? To nose through cold dirt and herbal shards? The aeronautics of such a leap from a cat who is shaped more like a diving bell than an F-22 would seem to be fanciful. And even if dear Gato had thudded to a safe if not soft landing, would he know to contain his curiosity not to . . . look over . . . even venture over . . . the railing?

It was too horrible to contemplate. But necessary. Slippered feet on cold concrete, we stepped out to peer over the railing, seven floors down. *Whew.* No sign that our momentous cat had fallen. Caroline surveyed the landscape, and within a few moments noticed a protuberant white blur presiding over a planter across the way. *Cat ahoy!* Gato Blanco had apparently made his way, step by step, paw pad by paw pad, planter by planter, from our perch above the city to one on the other side of the apartment building, facing ours. We held ourselves back from waving so the gregarious Gato would not raise a paw from his sinecure to wave back, and perhaps lose his grip on the soil of a planter and . . .

He prowled back, planter by planter, slowly and majestically, toward our balcony. It was like watching a great ship approach its mooring. But we worried that some kind of distraction—a bird might flap by, or a dog's bark rattle his composure—would tip Gato over the edge of a planter. Thankfully, he arrived at our perch without diversion or disturbance, in one, whole, hefty, fluffy presence.

You know you love the animals in your life when they can put your heart in your throat.

WORM WORLD

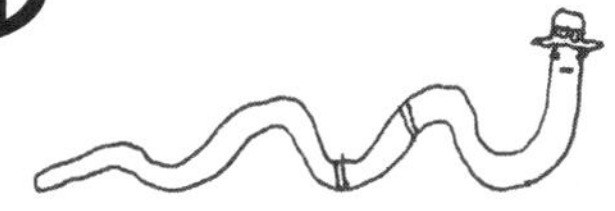

Worms are the world's essential citizens. They dine on what's gone (including us, when the time comes) and aerate the earth, which helps all things grow. Their "castings" (which a lot of us might call "worm poo") nourish the soil with nitrogen, phosphorus, and other rejuvenating bacteria (a phrase that does not come naturally to me). Then, in a lifetime gift to our planet, worms that burrow, wriggle, and otherwise frolic in the soil also incite the interest of birds, frogs, and hedgehogs.

Feasts ensue. They are, to be sure, one-sided. But as Charles Darwin once observed of worms, "It may be doubted whether there are many other animals which have played so important a part in the history of the world, as have these lowly organised creatures."

I have retained his Anglo *s* in "organised" just to make it clear that this is the product of research. Darwin even put worms in his piano to see if they could hear. They did react to the vibrations, but no worm has composed a symphony—so far.

You might ask, What is a worm colony doing in a bin on our balcony?

They were invited. Well, *ordered* might be a more precise way to phrase it, as their commonwealth of worms were already wriggling, dining, mating, and rejuvenating the soil of their society that was wrapped inside a packing crate when it was delivered to our apartment.

Caroline cares lovingly for the worms and deploys their castings into the flower boxes on our balcony to nourish herbs and flowers. Basil and tarragon flourish, to be trimmed and plopped onto our plates. One spring night when Caroline popped the top on their black rubberized bin on our balcony, I realized the worms, too, had wormed themselves into our lives.

We see the worms wiggle, slither, shimmy, and writhe in what seems like sheer happiness. I have bestowed on them the names of local public radio stations and hail them saying: "Hello, WBEZ! Hello, WBUR, WNYC, KCRW, and KUT! Hello, Ideastream—Cleveland rocks! Hello, KQED!" I have convinced myself that their wiggling in return is a sign of personal recognition.

Caroline sometimes says that she is not feeding our family so much as preparing scraps for the worms. She bestows table scraps of corn kernels, brussels sprouts, and kale on our worms. She showers them with shredded envelopes, old credit card statements, and shards of the Sunday newspapers, all moistened into a mulch. As she says, "Who wouldn't love the humble worm? They ask so little and do so much. Quiet, unseen, purposeful."

I like to think I can hear our worms chowing down. Do I even hear a call for a wine list? "Uh, what goes best with old, sticky rice, monsieur?" Strike up the café music . . .

We cannot quite bring ourselves to include our worms when people ask, "What pets do you have?" But Caroline and our daughters bring blankets out to the balcony to enrobe and warm the worms in their bin on the coldest nights. And Daisy certainly considers the denizens of the bin to be rivals for attention. Daisy often accompanies Caroline outside when she serves the worms the scraps and shreds she has saved for them. When she pops the top of their worm-i-verse and calls out sweetly, "Hello, *mes choux!*" Daisy barks and snarls. She feels that sweet, honeyed voice is a gift to be conferred only on her. And possibly our daughters. And maybe sometimes on our cat and hamster. But those burrowing invertebrates on our balcony? They don't even have backbones!

Our worms are not our pets; and yet, they are *ours*. They are part of what we want to widen our hearts to include in what we care about, day by day, in the most direct and per- sonal way. How are they? Do they have enough to eat? Are they safe? Are they happy? Would they like some cabbage scraps or a quilt tonight?

DINING WITH DAISY

We go to restaurants freely with Daisy in France, which makes her wonder why American establishments are so . . . snobbish. She believes that the ambiance (she says it with the French pronunciation, of course, lightly kissing the final *sss* sound with her tongue) of any restaurant is improved by the presence of a dog or cat, and asks, "Can you say the same of all people?" I must admit, she makes me think.

Sometimes she'll come out with me in the early morning in France, and sit under a café table while I suck up, American-style, a *double expresso* and a slice of baguette. She does not scramble up on the table for a bite. She does not beg, under the table, for scraps. She sits strategically by my right elbow, knowing that I will typically turn in that direction to take a bite, which will send enough crumbs drifting down to keep her engaged until the next bite.

Daisy does not need the crumbs for nourishment, but she welcomes the sport of crumb-gobbling. She is, in fact, a World Cup star at crumb-gobbling.

Some days, we'll stop for lunch, and she'll look up, seemingly irked, to hear me order just a gazpacho. Thankfully for us both, a baguette typically rests alongside. Daisy may be more familiar with the menu at some of our favorite places than I am. She seems to register no excitement at the sound of someone ordering oysters or mussels. There are no crumbs to be harvested from shellfish. But at the utterance of "baguette," Daisy assumes gobbling stance.

We don't pay much mind to restaurant rating sites, but we do favor restaurants that welcome Daisy as a member of the family. The pizza spot downstairs in our apartment building in the US, for example, which lets her linger as we chat with neighbors, or the rotisserie spot in France where they recognize that ancestors of Daisy once hunted for the birds who turn on their grills.

A few years ago, we were in Rouen, Normandy, for the sad occasion of a memorial for my wonderful mother-in-law, Marie-Amélie Richard. Daisy was with us, of course. But she spent much of the day sequestered in our rented car, so as not to tempt the large, assertive farm dogs who ruled the property. It was an afternoon of laughs, wet eyes, and hugs. I kept imagining my mother-in-law as a little girl, growing up with her brothers and sisters in the cellar of that farmhouse, sleeping between boxes and barrels on a hard floor, while Nazi staff officers occupied their living room and bedrooms in the house above. Marie-Amélie had survived, gone on, and grown up. She never ceased to look for ways to laugh, and her children inhaled and inherited her effervescence. I thought of the way she'd smile to sprinkle feed for her beloved chickens: "Here you go, my sweet peas!" I thought of how she told us her devoted dog, Merlot, was so endearing he would be stolen by some band of international dog thieves. "A dog so cute . . ." she used to caution.

We came back late to our hotel in the center of town. We carried the sadness of the day, but also giggled with family gossip. Daisy pulled on her leash. Dogs change our moods according to what they need, and that helps us turn a page. We realized we were all hungry.

A few tourists lingered in the town's market square, drawn to see the spot where Joan of Arc was so ignobly burned at the stake in 1431. Much of the square had shut down and gone dark, but we saw a light over an entryway: *Kebabs et Frites*. They were still open. Kebabs, *frites*, and ice cream for our daughters. And a man who ran the stand smiled to see Daisy, bouncing between our daughters, delighted by the sight and scents of so much food out in the open. He carved some morsels of gyros for Daisy onto a small plate and bestowed it to her on the floor with a flourish, as if presenting foie gras to a European monarch. It was one of those moments when I realized all over again that here we were, from all different places around the world, and all different backgrounds. But anyone seeing us as they passed the restaurant on the square on a summer's night would see our smiles and know that that we were a family, parents, daughters, and dog, gobbling kebabs and laughing.

DAISY ON NORMANDY BEACH

Our family walks along the beach almost every morning and night when we're in Normandy. We unhook Daisy from her leash and let her run up and down the beach, which is mostly empty, and always grand and magisterial. There are forts and castles along the sea, but now made of sand. History hangs in the air. Daisy and our daughters romp freely. We like to think that's what history has done.

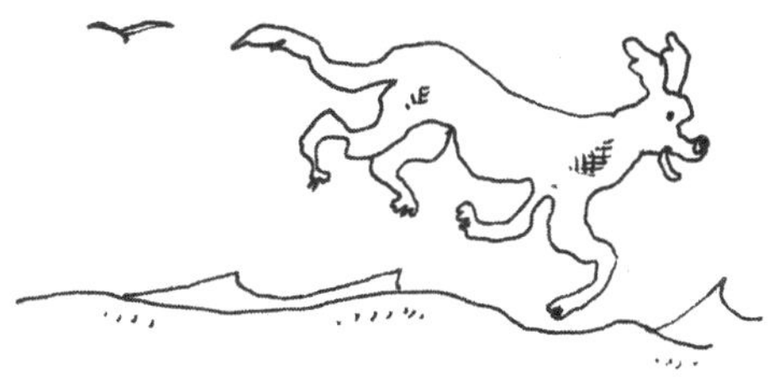

SLOGANS AND RALLYING CRIES

Over time, I have sketched out some slogans for the animals in our lives to herald their everyday existence.

Daisy might have a scarf wound around her shoulders:

CUTE IS CURRENCY

For Gato Blanco, our enormous fluffy foster cat, perhaps a nameplate below the box—any rectangular object—he appropriates for a nap:

I SHED, THEREFORE I AM

For Bagel, our small hamster, perhaps a neon crawl-sign to roll across the Hamster Dome in our daughter's bedroom:

SMALL, UNSEEN, BUT SPRINTING

And for the worms who live and work in the black tub of a bin on our balcony, I imagine a banner, unfurled and waving in the breeze, to proclaim to all:

YES, I'M SLIMY. BUT WHAT DO YOU
DO FOR THE ENVIRONMENT?

And so our older daughter has dubbed our worm-land
"the Slimons."

IGNORANCE IS BLESSED

A friend who is an artist paid a visit to our family recently, and Daisy loved to snuggle and rest in her arms, and to be picked up so their faces were brought together, nose to snout.

"You know why they love that, don't you?" asked our accomplished friend. "When they're puppies, their mothers regurgitate food into their mouths. We think our dogs are smiling, but they've actually been weaned and conditioned to think that when we look into their little faces, we're going to regurgitate food into their mouths."

Well, I've been weaned and conditioned to think that Daisy is smiling at me. I will simply ignore any other explanation.

GATO, DESTROYER OF WORLDS

Ever since work-from-home took hold, I've been interviewing people a couple of days a week from a library table in my home office that suddenly had to accommodate a second laptop, a second screen, a keyboard, a microphone, and machines and terminals with mystifying coded names that highly skilled broadcast engineers need to talk me through to operate. They sound like air traffic controllers in a movie, trying to guide a passenger into landing a 747 after all the pilots are felled by stomach poisoning. "Okay, Scott," they say, "can you see IP34? Look for IP34! No, *don't press that blue switch!*"

Gato loves to join in. I think he hears me yammering, often pleasantly, with some unseen author, performer, or politician, and figures that our conversational group is incomplete without him. He pulls up at my feet as I sit at the mic, then looks up. *I'm invited, right?* Taking care to keep my mouth in range of the microphone, I turn my knees so that Gato can leap into my lap, *oomph*, with a thud for which I hold my breath. As our guest declaims about their latest novel, film, interest, or cause, Gato clenches and unclenches the claws in his paws and looks up again to catch my eyes. *Why are you talking into that foamy, squishy thing when I'm right here?* He next presses his pink nose into the soft gray foam that enfolds the mic. *Hey there! Cat here! And I've got some questions, Senator!* I squeeze Gato slightly softly, to signal, or so I think, that now would not be the best time to meow, well, like a cat.

And so Gato often climbs from my lap onto my broadcast table. It is an old Chicago Public Library table, currently embellished (cluttered is another word I've heard) with family photos and mementos that didn't make the cut for display downstairs, knickknacks, writing instruments, postcards, and prayer cards. He slides past a framed photo of our daughters, snapped at an orphanage in China, a Mass card of Pope Francis from a Vatican gift shop, and another old Mass card from my mother's bedside collection, offering the Unfailing Prayer of St. Anthony.

Gato flips the prayer from its place with a swipe of his tail. *Swish!* Then he saunters past a propped-up postcard of a zebra, with a Father's Day note from our daughters on the flip side, past the photo of my mother and my late stepfather, Ralph, and then another from Ralph's seventy-fifth birthday party, and my mother's State of Illinois ID card, which Gato knocks down with another flourish of his tail. *Swish!* Then he nudges over my bronze peacock shoehorn from a market in Jaipur. *Ding!* Then he slaps over a small, stony bust of St. Simon from a souvenir shop in Sevilla with a paw—*clang!*—on his way to nuzzle thumbnail grade school pictures of our daughters, held by a butterfly clip and a baby bracelet, and a St. Francis de Sales prayer card from their old school from which I often recite before beginning a day of interviews. "Help me to conduct myself during this day in a manner most pleasing to you." *Thwap!* A Mass card of St. Francis, with birds lighting gently on his arms, is just alongside, and dismissed with equal alacrity. *Thwack!*

I quietly hold out a hand as I listen under a headset to whomever I am interviewing, briefly slowing Gato's swaggering cross from stage right to stage left. His tail continues to dart and sway like a dancing serpent, beguiling, musical, and unpredictable. There's another Mass card (my mother kept quite a collection) declaring a Prayer for my Pet. It goes, "We especially thank You for giving us our pets who are our friends and bring us so much joy in life. Their presence very often helps us get through trying times."

Gato Blanco's tail just goes *thwack!*

At this point in the interview, someone is confessing why they engineered the robbery of the National Bank of Spain, or what it felt like to sell a million recordings, and I must lean back to get close to the mic to remark, "Huh?" or "Why?" Gato takes the opportunity to nose a small clock, a snow globe from France, and a mug of pencils, then decides there is something not quite right with the way they look where they are. So he scrunches his small, strong, white woolly head against the clock and pushes it against the pencil mug, and against the snow globe. In an instant—*crash! splat! thonk!*—they are felled, as if a tornado had just swirled by. And in a way, it has.

Our guest will often say something like, "Excuse me, but is everything . . . all right?" I suppose I could say, "I am so sorry, that was just a technical problem," but I don't want our engineers to have to take responsibility, or look for a technical problem when there is none, only Gato Blanco, Destroyer of Worlds. And so I tell all, "I'm sorry. Our cat, Gato, just knocked something over."

Some awfully big names, and many understanding people, have reacted by saying, "Oh, that's okay. Are they all right? What's their name? Can I say hello?"

I settle back in front of the mic to recover with another question. Gato plops his midriff onto the computer mouse and sets off lights, flashes, and havoc on the screen, which is thankfully, for the moment, silent.

TOSCANINI WITH A TAIL

Gato loves music. We often have light jazz, French standards, or show tunes playing in our household, and Gato seems to accept it as mood music: something he must endure until his name is called in the waiting room of a spa.

But he is stirred inside his fur-encircled heart by opera: the voice of Maria Callas especially.

Gato hears the opening to her soaring arias and his long, white, expressive tail rises, like a conductor taking the podium. Then, as La Divina sings Puccini's "O mio babbino caro," or Verdi's "I vesprei siciliani," his tail begins to dart, spiral, and sway. He snaps his tail to counterpoint staccato sections. He commands it to quiver through crescendos.

Leonard Bernstein used his baton sedately compared to the way Gato wields his tail through "O Scarpia, avanti a Dio!"

There are perhaps some utterly unexceptional scientific reasons for Gato's musical enthusiasms. Cats have highly sensitive hearing, over a larger range of frequencies than our poor human ears can detect. Gato might, in fact, be able to hear notes attained by the great Maria Callas that we never can. Even his whiskers can absorb music.

But other thoughts play in my mind, too. I like to imagine that, a number of generations back, a similarly opulently padded white cat may have been in residence at La Scala, in Milan: in 1904, specifically, as they prepared to mount the first production of *Madama Butterfly*. Giacomo Puccini made constant revisions to his masterwork as they moved toward the premiere. And the great singers of that time and stage complained that his changes were coming too quickly to be learned, rehearsed, and revised again.

"*Gesù Cristo!*" a great soprano protests, operatically, to her costar, the tenor. "How are we to keep up with all the changes? Even the great conductor Toscanini is confused!"

(And, no, I have no explanation for why the great soprano would begin the sentence in Italian, then finish it in English. But just try to work with me here, okay?)

"*Sì, il mio grande soprano,*" replies the tenor. "But there is a white cat—a cat of size and substance; the Monte Viso of cats, if you please—who has heard each performance through each change. He has reacted with visible *sensazione*. If only this cat could somehow be induced . . ."

"I will leave out a plate of cacio e pepe," the soprano assures him.

The next night is the premiere. The great Toscanini, of

course, is at the podium. But nearby, adorned in his own nature's bounty of white tie and tails (and perhaps licking a few last traces of cacio e pepe), is the feline opera aficionado whom La Scala employees have come to call Gatto Bianco.

Toscanini raises his baton. Gatto Bianco lifts his long white tail. The maestro nods to his protégé, and the first chords of "E soffitto e pareti" resound over the gilt balustrades and velvet walls of the world's greatest opera house. The rest, of course, is musical history.

A few cat generations, and maybe an unplanned ride by a curious cat inside a barrel in the hold of a Genoa-to-America cargo ship later, and Gato Blanco is accompanying La Divina in our midst.

THE ESCAPE ARTIST

Bagel, our older daughter's hamster, is about two inches long and half an inch wide, snoozes all day, and runs at night on an enclosed wheel. The squeaks prickle the exquisitely sensitive ears of our dog, Daisy, who sometimes stares up at Bagel's Plexiglass enclosed environs with an expression that is hard to read. Does she see Bagel as a disturber of her sleep—or a snack-in-training? As a family member—or a morsel?

In fact, both our dog and cat have had their chances.

Bagel lives, eats, poos, prowls, explores, exercises, romps, rests, and gambols in a kind of Colosseum Rodentia on a dresser in our daughter's room. Her environs are outfitted with that wheel, six wooden ramps, ledges, and stairs, all laid out, as Pierre L' Enfant might have planned it, on spongy grounds of confetti-like scraps of treated colored paper. There are large food and water troughs. Green pottery cacti sculptures stand up from the landscape.

Bagel's Hamster Dome is so extensive and opulently equipped, I've wondered if we shouldn't make it available for weddings.

And oh, her name? Bestowed by Elise, who was working at a deli. And Bagel soon began to fit the small, endearing animal who came so close to being delicious.

We had come to that hour of the night when we prepare to retire. Lights snapped off, last cups and glasses cleared, front door locked, and the humans in our household headed for the stairs and slumber.

Caroline . . . yelped. It was not an unbridled scream from a horror movie, but a yelp, held in her throat, as she stopped in astonishment and uncertainty. What to do, what to do?

Gato was on our stairs. He was fondling some dear little brown-and-white fluffy thing between his paws. *Awww* . . . It must be one of those little mouse toys we got him at the pet store! He loves it! How cute! But wait now . . . the little mouse . . . just kind of . . . *moved*! *Wait!* Do we have a mouse in our apartment? We had before. Gato trapped one shortly after his arrival in our family, and we laid out sticky traps in strategic spots so they would get stuck. But wait: maybe this is . . . a rat! I hear someone on the second floor had a rat. There are rats running out of the pizza place downstairs like DoorDash drivers. But wait: up there on the stairs. It's not a mouse, or a rat, it's . . . *Bagel!* Between Gato's paws! And the brown-and-white fur on her back is standing up because Gato . . . is *licking her*!

Is it love—or a foretaste of a canapé caught between his paws?

Hence the yelp I can translate here only as "Oooooyyyeee-oooowwww! Woo! Woo! Aaach!" It sounds even more alarming in French.

Most of us froze. But Caroline carefully . . . advanced. She says she caught a glimpse of Bagel's brown dot eyes, suddenly bulging to the size of quarters.

"I thought it would be more fun," she sensed Bagel saying, with chagrin, "to come out and play with the big kids!"

A cleaning had left the broad door to Bagel World flapping open. Mistakes were made. But Caroline advanced with finesse and surety. "Okay, Gato. Put down little Bagel gently and come here. Over here. We have treats for you. That's right. Good boy. That's a good boy. Put her right here. Goood boy!"

Caroline swept Bagel into her hands and against her chest for safekeeping. Good boy, Gato. Good girl, Bagel. Mission accomplished; crisis averted. Your hearts may resume beating . . .

🐾 🐾 🐾 🐾

Then, a few months later, Caroline and I were packed and ready to depart on a two-day trip. Both daughters were staying home, one for work, one for school, to look after our running mates in the family. We were saying goodbye, tossing out reminders with each hug. "Now don't forget to walk Daisy before you leave for work." "Check Gato's bowl before you go to school." "Look into Bagel World before you go to bed . . ." Each reminder was met with, "We know. We know!"

Daisy, meanwhile, seemed to be roving, nosing, and whining behind our standing suitcases. "Oh, we love you, too, Daisy," we hastened to add. "And you, too, Gato. And you, too, Bagel . . ."

Car service sent an alert. Parked downstairs, and would soon depart. Final farewell kisses. Daisy scrambled into the kitchen, barking. "She sees something under the stove," a daughter announced. "Go take a look," we advised. "Must be some kind of bug. Maybe a mouse." A daughter followed, flashlight on her phone shining bright.

We heard a scream. Then a heart-twisting cry, and tears. It was Bagel, sweet, tiny Bagel, stuck on her back, upside down, on a glue trap we'd slipped under the stove. Caroline ran to the kitchen. I ran to our daughter, who said Bagel wasn't moving. "We're not leaving," we announced. Caroline slid her hand below the stove to retrieve poor Bagel, unmoving, on her back, for burial, but then announced quietly, "I think, maybe, she's moving."

Tears gushed. But Caroline was deft and proficient. She plucked from the kitchen countertop a pair of scissors we used to slash open bags of frozen peas, pasta boxes, and tightly taped packages. She guided the scissors with exquisite French swordsmanship.

Then Paulina saw that the sharp blades were slicing uncomfortably close to Bagel's twitching back. Caroline took a firm, steadying breath and ripped Bagel's backside from the flat, gluey surface of the trap. She was freed, at the cost of just a few strands of fur and a slight limp in a wriggly little leg. She settled woozily within Caroline's hands, so our family could see that she had survived the ordeal. Then Caroline lifted her back into the friendly confines of her Hamster-Rama.

Our daughters were relieved and happy. Bagel survived and thrived, Gato stayed unflustered, and Daisy was hailed for sounding the alert with her barking, "Hey, hamster down, hamster down!" Caroline and I made our flight, and happily.

I have no scientific proof to offer when I say I have convinced myself that whatever natural appetites may spur Daisy and Gato to cast occasional hungry glances up at Bagel in her glass Rodentia Dome, they have had the chance to make a snack of her. And each time, they have elected just to bat her between their paws, playfully, or, when she was visibly stuck and helpless, call out for her rescue. I believe Daisy, Bagel, and Gato know they are family.

THE LONG HAUL 

There has been a couple in our apartment building named Pierre and Claire, who have lived together for seventy years. We encountered them often as they walked their dog, Véronique, and we would trade neighborly gossip in French and English.

Véronique died a few months ago. Claire and Pierre were disconsolate, but they took another dog into their lives within a few weeks: Penelope, a small, endearing, scruffy-haired terrier.

Naturally, some know-it-all neighbors whispered doubts. Claire and Pierre were in their late eighties. How could they take on all the responsibilities of a puppy? Feeding, walking, picking up after, and playing with her? And what becomes of Penelope in the event of their demise, which people in their eighties know may be only a little time ahead?

But then we'd see Pierre, smiling to be tugged along on walks by Penelope. We were just glad to see they had found one another, for whatever time they may have.

I do not doubt the facts of actuarial tables. But speaking as someone who lost a father young and who has covered wars, I don't think it's wise to get those numbers confused with the gift of bringing a pet into your life. If Pierre and Claire had decided not to get a dog in their later years, they would not have had the joy of Véronique alongside them for the last ten years.

Claire passed away recently. Other people in the building now help Pierre to walk and care for Penelope. Pierre reports that their dog still ranges around their apartment, looking for Claire; perhaps she always will. And when she tires of her search and decides to rest up for the night, Pierre says that she spreads out and makes herself comfortable on Claire's pillow, right next to him. In a way, they've become a trio again.

AND SO HOW WAS YOUR NIGHT?

It was that hour of the day when there is often a happy clatter in the kitchen, and the merry clangor off the walls of our daughters giggling. But I heard a screech and a groan from my wife, Caroline. There was—how to say this nicely?—a pile of spew on our staircase. And Daisy, our poodle, had scampered into her travel case (which we keep, unzipped, under a piano bench, precisely for those times she may need to seek a respite from us).

Daisy had a guilty countenance. Her head was sunk between her paws, her eyes were turned up, dewy and widening, her tail tucked. And there was another small pile in front of her.

Caroline reached into Daisy's case to offer comfort. Daisy snapped. *Grrr!* Then another sound entirely.

Scolding, bandaging, and delicate swearing followed. Then there was a family hunt to discover what might have been the source of her digestive distress. Were there cookie crumbs in the vicinity? An empty, licked-over bag that once held potato chips? A school lunchbox hauled down from a counter for its leftovers? Nothing surfaced.

We congregated at the dinner table to worry. We all recalled how Daisy had once gobbled down half an Eli's of Chicago chocolate cheesecake we had left on a table. A speedy trek to an all-night vet followed, to induce what needed to be done.

"But she's vomiting on her own now," Caroline told us. "That's probably good." Daisy, seeking comfort as well as to atone for her snap, sat on Caroline's lap. Our dog's eyes were drowsy from her labors. "Maybe she ate something outside," we all guessed. When we walked Daisy outside, we saw grass, streets, swaying trees, and flowers. But from her height of eight inches above the ground, Daisy saw a city teeming with crumbs, bugs, rats, bird ordure, and birds who had flown into buildings and been left splat on the sidewalk. She nosed into it all.

Caroline moved her plate slightly so that Daisy could rest her snout on our dining room table. It was a time for her to feel a part of us.

Gato Blanco, our cat, sauntered by, as if to announce to Daisy, "Well, some of us are feeling fine!"

We ate, we worried, we walked Daisy one more time and prepared to go to bed. We opened a window slightly to welcome the cool air of an autumn night. Daisy claimed her place atop the bed in which Caroline and I sleep. Our daughters congregated to say good night with coos, cuddles, and last looks of concern. We settled in. The night breeze gently rustled over us. Sleep began to fall like a gentle cloak.

And then Caroline screeched.

I bolted upright in the dark, as if alerted by a siren. Gato Blanco, who is Falstaffian both in width and wit, had somehow managed to half slither through the thin slit of open window and was halfway out on a ledge. We hadn't rolled a screen into place. He was taking the opportunity less to escape than to explore. But the risks of peril on a ledge, late at night, eight floors above city streets, are legion. Within half a second, I envisioned them all: Gato, going *plunk* through the glass roof of a passing car; Gato, trying to land on his feet and discovering his soft paw pads weren't quite up to meeting hard concrete; our daughters, shocked and sobbing; my wife and I feeling bereft and negligent.

Caroline bounded from our bed. She launched herself toward Gato's hind legs and latched onto him, as if grabbing the handle of a baby carriage about to head over a cliff in an old cartoon. If Gato so much as squeaked, it was swallowed by the late-night din of the city outside. But he had the good sense to know when he had encountered a *force majeure*. With the magical skill he had somehow developed, Gato slenderized himself to slip back through the slit of the open window. He settled onto the ground as Caroline slammed the window shut. Cheers and sighs of relief ensued all around.

Where were we? Oh yes, bedtime. Daisy, still slowed by what we figured to be stomach distress, took up her position on our bed. If her distress erupted again that night, well, at least we would be close. *Yuck.* Gato Blanco, no doubt oblivious to the consternation of which he had been the source, sauntered off to one of our daughters' bedrooms. The night was young! Surely they would sneak a watching of something, while he settled alongside, dreams dancing in his sage white head, while the city below went on night shift. We felt anxious and amused, relieved and exhausted, tired and grateful. Daisy digested successfully, Gato came back from the brink, Bagel, our hamster, thrummed on her wheel for a little late-night gymnastics, and our daughters had another story to take along in life. Surrounded by our animals, we laughed ourselves off to sleep.

DAISY EYES

It's that morning of the week when Caroline and I include a stop at a coffee shop while walking Daisy. We get coffee drinks for us and banana bread to share, and in that we invite Daisy. But when we made our stop one recent morning, Caroline reminded me of the digestion problems Daisy has been suffering. Banana bread would not be advised. In fact, all banana bread would be forbidden on this day, for Daisy's own sake.

(Come to think of it, we finish a lot of sentences that way.)

I stood at the counter waiting for our drinks to be topped off, and avidly avoided what I knew would be Daisy's anxious, anticipatory gaze. I came out with a cup in each hand but no little brown bag, redolent with the scent of banana bread. I could see Daisy sniff, to no avail. She examined my hands exhaustively, then pulled back her snout in disappointment. My heart sank. Daisy then sat in front of me and fixed me with the kind of stare that Romeo trained on Juliet, the same kind of gaze that Yuri Zhivago fastened on Lara across the Russian steppes. Daisy's eyes brimmed with trust, dew, and adoration. They were bursting, brown, wet, and imploring. Her eyes bore into my heart like a chiseled drill bit.

And then, Daisy glanced down and saw crumbs. Croissant flakes, smidgens of granola, and perhaps specks of muffin crumbs, fallen from the lips of previous customers, probably while chatting over lattes about something on Netflix. But Daisy had no reason not to think those pastry specks hadn't been left just for her. Our animals hold hopes for us, but not grudges. They show us how sometimes the gift to keep going isn't to remember, but to forget.

MARJAN OF KABUL

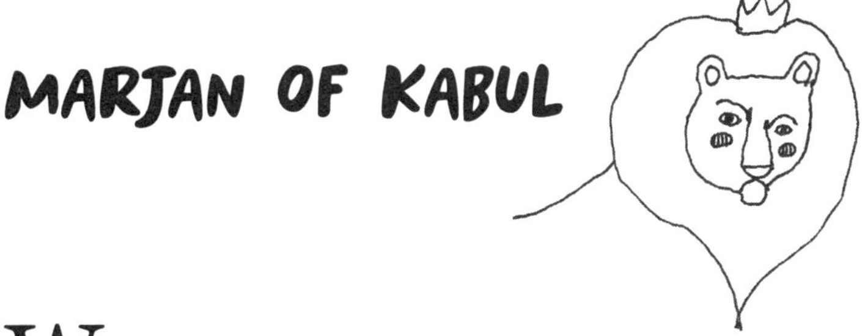

We heard about Marjan almost as soon as producer Peter Breslow and I reached Kabul, as the Taliban retreated in December 2001. Marjan was the Lion of Kabul, given as a gift by the Cologne Zoo in 1978. The celebrated lion had lived through warlords, uprisings, civil wars, religious strife, Soviet occupation, and the barbarity of Taliban rule.

In 1995, locals told us, a Pashtun soldier strode into Marjan's den at the zoo and began to taunt him, sneering, "I am the real king of the jungle!" The soldier (if that's quite the word here) also began to paw, and pretended to mount Chucha, the lioness who shared Marjan's confines. His hoax was cruel, dumb, and costly. Marjan sprang to Chucha's defense. He corrected the soldier's assertion of authority in the way lions tend to do, with a slash of his claws into the man and a bite of his arm. The Pashtun warrior (a term I don't like to apply to a man who would taunt an animal, but God rest his soul) died from his wounds. The soldier's brother reportedly returned the next day and rolled a grenade into Marjan's cage.

Marjan lost an eye. His mane had been scorched. He was left deaf from the blast. But blinded, hobbled, and burned, the Lion of Kabul still seemed to retain his regal bearing as he looked out over the city that had sheltered him, and came to symbolize for many the resilience of the Afghan people.

But perhaps exhausted from his mission, Marjan died just after the Taliban withdrew in January 2002. Veterinarians from the British army told us he had simply run out of life; given all he had survived, that was almost something to celebrate. I remember thinking that morning, as we arrived at the zoo, it was as if Marjan had been holding on for better times to depart the stage.

Zoo workers, who were also survivors, told us that day how chimps and camels in the zoo couldn't take shelter, or run from shells and bullets. Many died where they lived, on the grounds on which they had made their lives as best they could. Of course, zoo workers were also killed by bombs and bullets, on the grounds on which they had given their lives for a love of animals. Both humans and animals ran out of food. Imagining their last days, hungry, weak, and under attack, was unbearable, even in the midst of war.

When we arrived to memorialize Marjan, we saw just a few turkeys, owls, a cute baby bunny, and a scar-nosed little macaque in residence at the zoo. Some had survived in the homes of zookeepers, and a few were farm animals filling in for zoo exhibits, so as not to disappoint families who were beginning to wander back onto the zoo grounds for some signs that life was returning to the city. A man named Farouk had brought his two-year-old daughter. The ringing of her laughter sounded as gorgeous as wind chimes across the frozen and snowy zoo grounds. But Farouk recalled happier times. He sat down with us to watch his daughter scamper. "It feels like a graveyard," he told us. "And so I feel like mourning." At a time when so many in Afghanistan lived in fear and loss, Marjan had roared for life.

MAKING ROUNDS

To watch our animals as they sleep touches something in our hearts. It's when they seem to declare with each breath, "I belong here. I feel safe here. And here is wherever *you* are."

Each of our animals has had different nocturnal routines, as, I suppose, have we, depending on the circumstances of our lives.

Lenore, a small Mexican cat I had when on my own, would reach a point each night, between the news and *Nightline*, where she would perch beside me on the couch and issue a loud, cranky cry that it was time to retire. Mostly, I complied.

Leona, our little orange British cat who came with me into married life, had a nightly *divertissement* with Caroline. She would wait until Caroline had slipped out of her shoes or slippers, then slide behind a door, only to spring out and nip at her ankles when she walked by. "Yeow!" Caroline would yelp, and then giggle, like the sound of little popping bubbles. Leona would bound back, then spring forward, her soft paws encircling Caroline's ankles, to take another nibble. It was affectionate and playful, but determined. I used to suggest that some old Anglo-Franco rivalries from the Hundred Years' War had flared inside Leona's stout little British heart. But after a few minutes of play, she would retire to our bed, which was her bed, and sleep pointedly between the two of us.

Then our daughters came into our lives. And Leona began to develop another vital role in our nighttime routines.

Caroline, Elise, Paulina, and Leona and I would often sit as a family on the living room couch. Caroline would brush Leona with a steel comb. Our daughters would come and go, pull themselves up, jump off, and toddle off elsewhere in the living room to play with dolls, wooden trains, stuffed horses. The time would arrive for Paulina to be put to bed. We would carry her to it, and Leona would follow, falling in with our steps. Then there would be stories, laughs, sometimes cries, and kisses, while Leona looked on from a corner of the bed, as if keeping tabs. *Do you know what you're doing? Do you really want to sing another one of those silly songs?*

In time, we parents would depart. Leona would stay, nestling in slightly more, pink nose against the curl of a cover. A few minutes later, Elise would amble by, us parents trailing. When she was tucked abed, we would hear Leona turn the corner, sometimes announcing her arrival with a cry. She would take a slight running jump to spring onto a bare corner of Elise's bed, where she'd listen to a few more songs and stories, and stay on the swells of a crumpled cover to see our older daughter into sleep, as she had seen our younger one. Leona was our daughters' lookout, their sentry, their protector and companion. She was their kith and kin.

Leona would then launch herself onto our slightly higher bed later that night, right after we slipped between the covers, spacing herself at first impartially between us. But sometime in the night, often around 3 a.m., I'd feel a slightly moist, slightly scratchy tickle in the corner of an eye. I might twitch and turn slightly, then feel another light, tenuous touch from Leona's bristly tongue. In time, I began to recognize: it was my cue. Leona had done her work. I was being summoned to do mine.

I would slide my legs out from under the covers, sit up, take Leona into my arms, and then pad, barefoot, into the kitchen. Her bowl was in a corner. I would sprinkle in a handful of snacks. I'd pad back to bed, and soon Leona would leap back up. She would slip under my right arm and shoulder and settle in for the last couple of hours of sleep for us both.

When I traveled, Leona would let Caroline sleep without interruption. I thought it was because Leona knew that Caroline might not be nearly so game to fetch her a treat, but Caroline said, "It's not about the treat. It's a game you two have."

When Daisy entered our lives, we purchased a dog bed. It is oval-shaped, fluffy, and inviting, and still at the foot of our bed. Sometimes it holds a foam roller, used in home exercises. Sometimes it holds a few pairs of shoes, as it's hefted onto our bed during vacuuming. Our dog bed, however, has almost never held Daisy. Now that I think of it, how and why would Daisy even consider a bed? Why sleep alone, in some kind of solitary faux-furred oval, when you can slip in between two warm human companions for the night?

She favors Caroline's side, by the way—and who wouldn't?—but occasionally veers over to mine.

On some occasions, Daisy will be abducted by one of our daughters, typically at a time when they could use the reassurance of her company. We grouse theatrically that we have been targeted by thieves. But of course, we're only delighted that our daughters should turn to Daisy for companionship (though Caroline and I are often cheered to discover that sometime in the dark of night, Daisy will have crept back between us, after missionary work with our daughters).

Now and then, we are stirred halfway out of sleep to hear Daisy seeming to dig at a spot in our bedclothes. Research suggests this is behavior inherited from her wolf ancestors, who were eager to bury food and carve out shelter. But only once have we discovered Daisy burying food in our bed (it was the crisp end of a baguette, in France). Her idea of "hunting" is to wait below me as I snack to pounce on what I spill. And as for shelter, she now prefers cotton sheets to dirt. Daisy flails and paws for a minute, then sinks back down onto the top of our down comforter. Soon she—and we—are back to slumber.

Gato Blanco, meanwhile, usually takes up a post on the corner of our younger daughter's bed, where he rests his chin on his paws to sleep, looking sphynx-like as he gazes at her royal presence.

There are moments I wake up in the night and feel moved to check on each of us in that continuing collaboration that is our family: Caroline at my side, Daisy between us, Elise abed down a hall, where we can hear a slight rustling from Bagel racing on her wheel, and Gato, in repose in the province of Paulina. There is quiet, closeness, and peace in a moment that I know is at once utterly ordinary and altogether perfect.

But we have strict rules about pets on our dining room table. They are not widely observed.

MIDDLE OF THE NIGHT

Gato paws at the door to Paulina's room.

She is asleep. So are her parents. But we hear Gato's cries and whimpers. There is a second entrance to her bedroom. Gato knows it. He has been known to use it. But that would entail walking down one flight of stairs, then up another, to get to her room, and it's the middle of the night. Why should someone of Gato's prominent profile resort to such gymnastics when he has house staff on call? He bleats, whines, and mewls.

"Cat?" Caroline calls out. Then, "Cat!" a little more sharply. Finally she utters a French curse, quietly, and stalks out of our bed to turn the handle that opens the door to Paulina's lair, substantially more than one might do for other cats, because, of course, this is for Gato. He slips in, like an A-list celeb being admitted through a private entrance. Caroline leaves the door comfortably ajar behind him and returns to slumber, grumbling slightly. Gato curls up at the foot of Paulina, the person who so cherishes him.

He has trained us well.

OBEDIENCE TRAINING FOR CATS

There is no such thing.

And by the way, Gato has taken to sitting on the right arm of a chair in which I write, early every morning, including today. He squints. He settles in. He raises his head, which is my signal to scratch him at the back of his head, which I do. White fur floats, then falls into my coffee cup. Gato stares at the screen. *You can peck at that keyboard with your left hand,* I imagine him saying. *Use your right for scratching. Ah yes, there. Ah yes.*

CHEEKY

There are fewer vignettes of Bagel, our older daughter's hamster, in this scrapbook of our running mates, because she is at once the smallest and least visible (fur-covered) member of our family assemblage. It is hard to know when to sing out "Good morning!" to a nocturnal animal.

But we do occasionally congregate at night before Bagel's Hamster Basilica. Her business days seem to commence with exercise and a snack. Bagel whirrs on her wheel, her small legs blurring into a fizz of tan-and-white fur, her soft pink nose lifted into the wind from her wheel. Ah, exercise! Set the table! One of us places pellets of food in front of her, and Bagel advances. She slurps the beige buckshot of food into her mouth, and hoards the pellets in her cheeks for imminent transport to a network of lairs she has excavated in her speckled, spongy, polychromous grounds.

I tell myself that surely Bagel knows that we, her innkeepers, provide food at regular intervals. Then again, from Bagel's point of view, why take that chance? On her reversed schedule, she can hear our gripes. A subway runs late, traffic backs up, weather scrubs a flight, and her breakfast is *not* served.

Konrad Lorenz, Niko Tinbergen, and Karl von Frisch received the Nobel Prize in part for work that ventured the analysis that a large round head, big eyes, chubby cheeks, and plump shapes can set off something in us humans they call *kindchenschema*. It is said to be what moves us to exclaim, "How cute!" and kindles an instinct to care for whatever or whomsoever we encounter with such features.

So those dewy eyes are all a scheme?

But I am uplifted to read what Konrad Lorenz said in his Nobel lecture in 1973. It may reassure those of us who sense common traits between ourselves and the animals in our family that we are not fooling ourselves.

"When we speak of falling in love, of friendship, personal enmity or jealousy in these or other animals," said Lorenz, "we are not guilty of anthropomorphism. These terms refer to functionally-determined concepts, just as do the terms legs, wings, eyes and the names used for other bodily structures that have evolved independently in different phyla or animals. No one uses quotation marks when speaking or writing about the eyes or the legs of an insect or a crab, nor do we when discussing analogous behaviour patterns."

Which I guess is the way a Nobel laureate says: Don't look for reasons to dismiss empathy, caring, and the common cause we make with the animals in our lives.

ANIMAL INTERPRETER

I am the voice of the animals in our family. My wife and daughters might hear Daisy crunch her head against her bag of food stored off the kitchen and call, "Oh, look, she's hungry!" Or, "Not yet, Daisy! Another half hour!" But I am the one who tries to cast myself into her furry skin and wily mind and announce to all, in what I take to be Daisy's voice in human speech, "Ey, *ma famille*, it is 4 p.m., and I have been cute all day! It is tiring, *mais oui?* A great performer such as I deserves some of those nuggets that taste like coq au vin to me! And now! *Tout de suite!*"

These sentences are pronounced in good faith, but in a French accent Caroline finds torturous. She cringes to hear such outrageous intonation of the elegant language of her nation.

Yes, but . . . But Daisy is a French poodle. As journalists so often have to say these days, all I can do is report the facts.

The voice I had divined for our little British cat, Leona, sounded like someone from the charming gang of street rascals in the musical *Oliver!* "Righto, mate! Just a l'il scratch behind me ears now! At'll do nicely! Thanks, French lady! I loves ya!!"

Whereas all our Salman Fishdies have sounded like Cambridge men, civil but slightly haughty. "I say, old chaps," as I'd report their words, "those dry flakes you have spilled so lightly into my bowl: I should regard them as sustenance?"

I was convinced that my mother's cat, Ulysses, spoke to us in flat prairie tones, issuing small puffs of smoke above his formidable orange head. "Got another cee-gar and tumbler of whiskey for this field general of the apartment?" I thought he'd ask. "Methinks the rebs might be at hand. An ol' pat o' me stomach might help."

These days, Gato Blanco will customarily perch on the arm of a recliner in the office where I begin the day shortly after 5 a.m. "You sure that's quite the right word?" I intuit him saying in orotund tones as he looks at my screen. "I'd give that a little more thought." He'll often, against all apparent laws of aerodynamics, leap onto tables on which plants and flowers are stationed, theoretically beyond his reach. Yet I am sure he is saying, between bites, "Hey, thanks for leaving this out. A little roughage is good for the diet, right?"

But my pet interpretations are regarded with skepticism by my family.

And of course, each day I supply a running commentary for—*from*—Daisy. "Ey, *ma famille*, it is *midi*. I cannot use that green poo bag without your assistance, *n'est-ce pas?*"

Caroline, our daughters, and Daisy were at a horse barn in

California a while back and met someone who called herself a horse psychic and claimed she could read the thoughts of animals. My family found her professed expertise instantly more credible than mine. Our daughters brought Daisy before her and requested a consultation. The equine Uri Geller placed her hands on Daisy. She assured them she was in touch with our dog's deepest thoughts. She asked of our daughters, "Is there anything you'd like to ask her?"

"Yes," they replied. "Ask Daisy, 'What do you think of our father's imitation of your voice? Do you find it as irritating as we do?'"

The psychic pressed her hands onto Daisy and bent her head against hers, presumably to mine her deepest thoughts.

"Daisy says, 'It is not a good imitation of me,'" the animal psychic insisted Daisy had declared. "'My voice is nothing like that. But your father seems to enjoy it. So just let him have his fun.'"

The animal psychic is shrewd.

We often recount the ways in which we rearrange our daily lives to accommodate our animals. When we arise, when we run errands, arrange our meals, look after their needs for the night, and then slip off to sleep with them close by. Now and then we might recall that our animals shuffle around their lives for us, too.

HOW MANY LAB RATS DOES IT TAKE . . .

I did a PBS program once at an important medical research facility in which everyone involved, from research scientists to physicians to the facility's maintenance crews, was doing important work to alleviate human suffering. They had dedicated their lives to trying to save lives. Even if they had not yet found a cure for a destructive and lethal disease, they had helped bring about treatments and discoveries that might lead there.

It was during a walk down a hall to set up for an interview with a researcher that a press representative mentioned how "thousands and thousands" of rats in their labs were deliberately infected with the lethal disease for which the facility was working to find a cure. Of course, those rats had died.

"Thousands and thousands?" I asked. Even then, I found my ignorance startling.

"Oh yes," she said. "Every one, of course, more or less." She must have read the shock on my face. "That's their job. Even if they survive, we have to section their organs and tissues." As my face must have crumpled more, she added, with absolute friendliness, "I don't even want to tell you about the hamsters."

I disguise some details now because I am grateful that the facility opened their research to us. Decades later, there is still no cure for the disease they were so assiduously working to subdue. I know that can be the nature of the most accomplished scientific research and enterprise. Yet I have had to keep myself from trying to calculate how many lab animals have been bred not just to die in such research, but to deliberately suffer the agonies of a puzzling and incurable disease for our human interests.

My feelings are fraught with contradictions. I take several medications a day that keep me alive and functioning. No doubt they have been developed through experimentation on animals. I'm grateful for each and every one (the medications, and the animals).

I can avoid using shampoos or toothpaste that rely on animal testing. But I cannot avoid medicines used to lower blood pressure or cholesterol.

If one million lab rats died in research that leads to a breakthrough in the treatment of cancer, AIDS, stroke, Parkinson's, ALS, COVID, mpox, or Ebola, I'd say: That's tough to hear. But I can accept the loss of a million lab rats to potentially save hundreds of millions of human lives.

I have a harder time knowing this: more than *a hundred million* rats die each year in American scientific laboratories.

You do not have to think of lab rats as having the same understanding, sentience, personality, or intelligence you impute to a beloved dog or cat to find yourself uncomfortable with the enormous numbers of rats and other animals who (and I use that pronoun purposely) die each year in research. They do not die from being hunted by another animal for food, or from lack of food. They do not lose their lives in the tough business of living. They die as part of the costs of a deliberate human enterprise—scientific research—that is crucial to pursue, even as it does not have a reliable return or result.

I am glad to learn that in recent years there have been advances in cell research and computer modeling that can spare rats and other feeling animals from being deliberately and scientifically subjected to the pain, indignity, and certain death of using animals for medical research. Someday, I'm pretty sure we'll look back on our use of animals in this way as something brutal.

CURLING UP

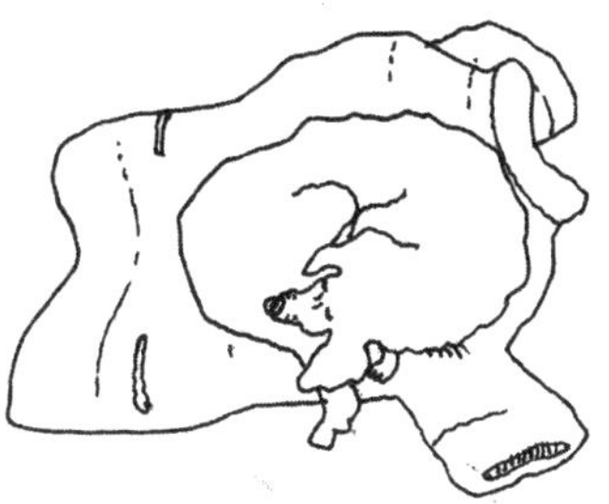

November comes and I shake out a puffy gray coat I got a few years ago for morning jaunts and errands. The coat is lined with a radiant emergency orange interior. According to the sign I recall on the rack, it is the same model of coat worn by Canadian polar explorers. Should I ever be stranded in a blinding white arctic wilderness and need to signal a search helicopter churning high overhead, I could just roll up a sleeve. A sliver of orange will be a beacon.

I used to stand up the coat in a corner of our entrance after morning rounds. But by midmorning, Daisy would nudge it into a heap and curl up in the center: a gray poodle resting on an impromptu orange pillow. These days, I just come through the door and lay out the coat, orange side up. Daisy snacks, sips, then ambles over to rest in the folds of our coat. Search helicopter, return to base.

THE KINGDOM OF GATO

Gato Blanco has claimed a kingdom in the realm of our apartment. We inherited a pool table when we moved in, which we planned to have removed. But when we inquired about the cost of moving a pool table out of the building, the quoted price inspired us to decide, "Well, why don't we just play pool?" Our daughters, thanks to a few videos and dedicated play, became so accomplished I began to hail them as "the Pros from Guangzhou."

The table could also be converted to play Ping-Pong. Some of their friends preferred that. But our daughters and their friends grew older and got drawn off by video games, which could be played with pals across town and across the world. The Ping-Pong top stayed on the large table, and all that flat, upholstered space became a congenial landing spot for the abundance of books we receive.

A kind of skyline began to take shape on our table as books were slipped out of mailing envelopes, boxes, and bags, and consigned to various stacks and towers. But where we might see piles of books, stacked according to those to be read soon, those to be read later, and those that made us wonder why they were sent, Gato saw his estate. He undertakes a procession there several times a day, leaping onto the table, spilling a trail of long white hairs, and blinking at piles of the newly unpacked and the waiting-to-be-reshelved. He saunters past, around, and between the towers, his tail swishing over book-spine billboards that blare Baldwin, Joyce, Jan Morris, and Patchett, James T. Farrell, Orwell, and Sontag. Occasionally he encounters a pen, or a Post-it, and thwacks it aside. Just for emphasis.

There was a small, flat place at the far end of the table that once held a box in which Caroline placed papers to be filed. Gato plopped into it when it was empty one day, as if it had been cleared for him. In a way, it had been. It is now the throne of Gato Blanco, where he presides over his subjects.

His Feline Excellency settles in, usually midmorning, when the sun can begin to shine off the river and into our windows. Gato surveys his domain. He squints as denizens—our family—approach him with favors, pats, and scratches. He rewards us by pressing his nose into our eager hands. He restores himself with quick naps. Quiet in the court!

It has occurred to me over time that Gato by now would have no reason whatsoever not to think that all our unpacking, stacking, and rearrangement must be just for his amusement. He's convinced us, too.

STRIPEY'S SAGA CONTINUES

Did you wonder? When we last left the little zebra who wandered into our family, Caroline had determined we had to find a way to reunite him with his herd, and I had decided that until we could do so, we had to find a way to bring him into the company of other zebras, which is not an easy task in most major American cities. Or really, any city. And so to continue . . .

We took a bus through the park in the early morning. A couple of passengers gave long looks at Stripey, then just looked back at their screens. One man called out, "Love your nature flicks!"

We got off at the zoo. I told the guards at the gate, "We have an exciting new addition for you."

The guards grunted and said that the zoo director would come out to meet us. We looked around for Stripey, and he was standing by the fence in front of the hippopotamus pond. The rails of the fence were black and ran up and down, and we had to look and look until we could see Stripey's ears twitch.

The zoo director wore a tan safari suit and thick brown boots, even though I think he only walked on the sidewalks that ran through the zoo.

"As you can see, we have a young zebra here," we told him. "We met him on the subway. He's quite handsome and intelligent, and we think he would get along very well with the other zebras here. We call him Stripey, so you wouldn't have to name him. He eats grass, so his diet is simple. Although we'd like permission to come by every week or so and bring him cheesecake. Mr. Director, meet Stripey."

I bowed in Stripey's direction, but the zoo director couldn't see him. Stripey twitched his ears, but to the zoo director, it just looked like a small white bird had landed on a lily pad in the hippopotamus pond. With his black-and-white stripes, Stripey just disappeared into the fence behind him.

The zoo director turned to talk into a small microphone clipped to the shoulder of his jacket.

"Security," he said. "Screwball at the hippo pond. We need backup."

We ran past the hippopotamus pond, then past the monkey house, then the Ice Kingdom, where the penguins lived, past snack stands with ice cream, cotton candy, and peanuts, souvenir stands selling stuffed pandas and plastic elephant snouts, and finally past the Great Ape Tropical Forest to reach the exit gate on the other side of the zoo.

"That was close," said Caroline when we were all finally on a bus headed home.

"He didn't look hard enough," I said. "You can't see a zebra unless you really, really look."

A woman on the bus came up to Stripey and said, "Excuse me, pal, but I think you missed a spot of cheesecake on your nose."

Paulina wiped it off with a tissue.

"Okay," I told our family the next morning, "I admit, my first bright idea didn't work. But I've got something else in mind."

We took the bus past downtown until we reached a large lot where a huge tent with red-and-white stripes had been put up. We walked into the tent and saw a couple of people juggling bowling pins, a woman in a spangled leotard walking on a thin wire stretched across the very top of the tent, and about a dozen clowns tumbling out of a small car.

A short man in a bright red jacket and a tall black hat greeted us.

"Hiya, hiya, hiya," he said. "I'm Ringmaster Kelly. Let me see your clown act."

"This is how I actually look," I told the ringmaster. "I'm not a clown."

"Oh, sorry, pal," he said. "Natural mistake."

"We have a little zebra here," Caroline explained. "Stripey."

"Cute little fella," said Kelly. "But cute is a dime a dozen in this biz. What does he do? Sing? Dance?"

I leaned over to Stripey and we conferred.

"Stripey does stand-up," I told him.

A couple of the clowns pulled out folding chairs and we sat in a half-circle around Stripey. The ringmaster pulled over a box for him to stand on. I took a pen from my pocket and held it like a microphone.

"Good evening, ladies and gentlemen," I said. "And now, the Rib-Tickler from the Serengeti, the Jester from the Great Migration, ladies and gentlemen, Stripey!"

We clapped and whistled while Stripey bowed, then spoke into the pen.

"Thank you, thank you, ladies and gentlemen," he began. "Just flew in from Africa—and boy, are my arms tired!"

The ringmaster cracked a small smile.

"Hey," asked Stripey, "anyone know how you fit six elephants into a convertible?"

"How?" shouted out Paulina.

"Three in the front and three in the back. Say, what do elephants do for luggage when they go on vacation?"

"No idea!" Caroline called out.

"They pack their trunks," said Stripey. "I got a million of 'em! Say, know why elephants don't play cards?"

"They can't hold cards?" I guessed.

"Nope," said Stripey. "Elephants don't play cards because of all the cheetahs."

This time, the ringmaster chortled. "Oh, that's a good one," he said.

"Why do elephants wear red toenail polish?" asked Stripey.

After we all spent a few seconds thinking and going, "Ah, err, uhm," Stripey said, "To hide in apple trees. Now, have you ever seen an elephant in an apple tree?"

"Never!" I shouted out. "Not one. Nada! Zippo!"

"Works, doesn't it?" said Stripey. "Hey, you've been a great audience. G'night!"

We stood up to clap, cheer, and whistle while Stripey bowed. The ringmaster clapped and smiled, too.

"You're good, kid," he told him. "Promising. But I got monkeys here who already tell great elephant jokes. Work up some new material and come see me in six months."

Stripey seemed sad on the bus ride home. I guess we all did. Paulina put an arm around his neck.

"You were great, Stripey," she told him. "Funniest ever."

"Six months is a long time," he said. "In six months, my herd will be all the way on the other side of the plain. My mother, my father, my friends. Every zebra I know."

Paulina fell asleep on Stripey's back that night. With her long black hair hanging down over his black-and-white stripes, you practically couldn't see her, sleeping and holding onto him.

❖ ❖ ❖ ❖

I don't want to give the (mostly happy) ending away. We have a lot of Stripey images in our apartment, cups, cards, platters, socks, and ties. He is not "real," of course. But his presence is with us, as much as any character from a novel or film that we take into our lives.

And of course, the most valuable fiction is spun from what is true. In the stories we tell, it is our daughters who can see Stripey first, when adult eyes are jaded and tired. It is our daughters who first reach out to bring that zebra, so artfully camouflaged into our cityscape, into our lives. There is a reason why so many storybook characters are created (ostensibly) for children, Piglet, Pooh, Paddington, Tigger, Miss Piggy, Simba, and the Velveteen Rabbit. A love of animals can help prepare and stretch our hearts for each other.

THE STRESS OF VETS

Nobody absorbs more of the loss of pets than veterinarians. Families bring kittens and puppies to them and place them in their arms and hands for scheduled shots and examinations, to remove thorns in their paws or help them disgorge unwisely digested treats. The vets see those pets through struggles with a whole catalog of infections, diseases, and vulnerabilities. They care for them the best they can, no matter what comes up—and out, if you please.

But even when the dogs, cats, rabbits, and birds we take into our lives enjoy long, happy lives, an end arrives. They have a clock for life that rolls by quicker than ours, and when it runs out, it is not a tragedy. It's life. But veterinarians live through this cycle time after time, day after day. They become doctors to care for animals, and often the last kind of care they can offer is to help the animals who have been so loved to take their last breaths.

In the summer of 2019, NPR producer Samantha Balaban and I were working on a series about the rise of suicide in the

United States. We reported on the increase especially among police officers and seniors. Then a web search for stories about suicide among *vets*, which we had entered to learn about military veterans, revealed that the Centers for Disease Control said *veterinarians* are more than twice as likely to die in an act of suicide than members of the general population.

There are some intensely practical reasons. Many veterinarians carry debts from medical school, but they don't earn the salaries of surgeons who operate on people. Many vets are relatively isolated, working in small practices where they must pay for rent and staff. They not only see a lot of their patients die, but hold them on their way. And vets, like police officers, have the means at hand to harm themselves.

We spent time with Dr. Carrie Jurney at her veterinarian practice in San Jose, California. She had been outspoken about the emotional struggles of her work, and explained that of her veterinary graduating class of eighty-six people, three had already died by their own hand.

"You know we fight death for a living," she told us. "We don't always get to win."

Her office during an early morning hummed with growls and meows, and the bleats and beeps of medical machines. We arrived shortly after the crew at her practice had performed a C-section to deliver four French bulldog puppies. Had the mother been living on her own, the puppies would not have been born safely. But here they were before us to greet the morning, wrapped snugly in towels, right before our eyes and beginning to open theirs, and napping and yapping. I asked, "Can I—is it okay if—I kiss them?" and got to put four light, quick smooches on their tiny, fuzzy heads.

"There are some perks to the work here," Dr. Jurney told us.

A local couple was waiting with their crumpled pumpernickel brown Rottweiler, Reuben. He weighed more than a hundred pounds. The night before had been a happy evening. The couple were just heading up the stairs for bed when they turned and noticed that Reuben hadn't tagged along. They stepped back down but Reuben stayed, unable to lift his legs. He looked up, softly whimpering. It was hard not to imagine how that sound would have pierced our own ears.

Dr. Jurney determined that they needed an MRI to diagnose Reuben, and her office staff lowered their shoulders and lifted their knees to shove him onto the board for the imaging machines. It was like trying to position a sack of cement.

Reuben's eyes grew wide and bewildered. If I had the effrontery to believe I could intuit the question clouding Reuben's eyes, the way I have claimed to be able to utter the thoughts of our animals, it would be something like, "What the . . . ? I thought you loved me!"

But veterinarians and their colleagues must actually try to communicate to their patients what might be unexplainable. How do you explain magnetic resonance imaging to a dog?

"One of the great ironies of my career is that I got into this because I love animals so much," Carrie Jurney told us. "There are not a lot of animals that are ever excited to see me anymore. And then we're doing weird things that they didn't get to consent to."

The MRI revealed painful knots on Reuben's spine. Dr. Jurney and her colleagues undertook immediate surgery. There was a mist of bone and blood as she drilled off the knots on Reuben's spine that had hardened around his nerves. "I think we did what we need to do tonight," she told us all, and called Reuben's couple. "I am going to get your baby tucked in," she told them, "and then I will call you in the morning."

It was one thirty in the morning after a long day and night, and Samantha Balaban and I felt graced and happy to have seen a gifted team of veterinary nurses and surgeons help a big, beloved dog to walk again, and to bring joy to the couple who loved him.

But a few days after our trip, I received a text message from Dr. Jurney: "Hey, Scott," she began. "I thought I should let you know we lost Reuben today. I have to be honest. This is gut-wrenching. You came to us to see why this job is hard. There is no better example than this. I am devastated. I've cried because my mind is with Reuben and his poor owners. Even though I know I did everything I could for him, I still wonder if I could have done more."

In a way, those of us who love our animals can see ways in which life's end may be a blessing for them at a certain time. The best veterinarians may be left to wonder if there was something they overlooked or one more thing they should have tried, or could have done, that might have kept a beloved animal going. I don't know how they do it, and don't know what our families would do without them.

CAT IN A BOX—OR SUITCASE

I know that when Gato Blanco plops himself into one of our suitcases as we pack, he is not really imploring us, "Please don't leave! What will I do without you? Who will feed me? Who will brush me? Who will sing to me? Who will leap onto your stomach in bed just as you're dozing off?" He is also not saying, "Hey, bring me along! We'll have a better time! Do you really want to spend all that time in a hotel room without me? You don't even know how to find movies without my help!"

Gato is simply fulfilling feline behavior. Cats are ambush predators. They look for confined spaces in which to hide and spring out onto unsuspecting prey.

But we know our animals, as they know us. We have accommodated ourselves to one another. We know how to reach into one another. And so when Gato crumples himself into an open suitcase, it's visibly to snooze, not to spring out onto—well, what, Gato? All your squeak toys? The trail of matzoh or cracker crumbs I may have managed to spill between the kitchen and the anteroom where a suitcase had been spread out? Or are you simply storing your sleek, leonine strength and grace to leap out of your slumber inside that suitcase and onto the dog bed you now share napping rights to with Daisy—for more snoozing?

This is where we begin to put ourselves into the minds of our animals. We can't hold ourselves back from assuming they can read our minds, even as they rarely know our words, and we can intuit their thoughts. In a way, it's a literary process: imagining and supposing from inside another's skin. Just a couple of trips we take might make our animals recognize that a suitcase, zipped open, presages the imminent departure of a family member. This upsets the world they know, in which they have carved out an irreplaceable position.

I've grown to think that our animals learn they cannot truly prevent us from departing. They don't nestle in our suitcases to declare, "You can't leave without me. Isn't it obvious?" But they learn how to press the valves and switches in our hearts that make us miss them. They have discovered how to curl up in front of us to remind us, and to spur us, to return, so that when we throw open the door upon coming back from Paris, a mountaintop in Nepal, or a run to a drugstore, our first words are often, "Gosh, I've missed you! I'm sooo glad to see you! Did you miss me?"

We'll take any semblance of a lick or tail wag as "Yes!"

DAISY ON THE ROAD

We travel with Daisy to those places where we might spend more than a few days, and find that bringing her along is easier and less worrisome than leaving her behind and trying to arrange for dog walkers and apartment sitters. Daisy turns out to be a fine traveler. She lounges on the small faux-fur rug in her travel case, gnaws on a toy, and often seems to enjoy the ride. She's with us, after all.

Or perhaps we're with her? Her attendants, which is to say our family, carry Daisy through the airport and onto the aircraft, shelter her from prying fans, and otherwise insulate her journey. When flight attendants ask, "Would you like a beverage?" I have been known to reply, "Our French poodle would like to see a wine list." Some attendants will just groan and say, "Tell her to check her seat card."

Daisy has been back and forth to France so much that she has a US location chip in one shoulder and an EU chip in another: she has become a true citizen of the world. Her required inoculations are recorded in a small book that matches the size of a passport, and so we refer to it as Daisy's passport. Our reveries are rewarded when we pass through EU passport control and a guard behind Plexiglass charged with protecting la République seems to survey her photo and instructs Daisy, "Turn left, Daisy, *oui?* Now right. *D'accord!* Yes, it eez you." Whew . . .

We flew back from a trip to the West Coast recently. San Francisco International Airport was a trial: long passages, long tram rides to gates, concourses closed for construction, we're sorry, thank you for your patience, you'll have to turn at Gate 76-Z to get back to Terminal 9. *Thank you for your patience.* We lifted Daisy from her coach so she could trot alongside us. At one point she pulled back, couldn't hold herself in, and left three souvenirs from the Bay Area on the concrete floor, dewy and bright.

French Scouts are always prepared. Caroline slipped a green bag from her jacket, scooped up Daisy's deposit, tied and plopped the bag into a refuse bin.

The flight was fine, even good. Daisy registered not a whimper. When we landed and boarded the people mover to the terminal, Daisy became our people charmer, appealing for pats, strokes, and smiles from people who had landed from all over the world.

But it was late at night. Our luggage was delayed. A voice from above and beyond the claim carousels explained that somehow, a container packed with bags from our flight had not been unloaded. We would have to wait even longer. Perhaps until a team of a dozen oxen could be trained to deliver the accumulation of suitcases, trunks, duffel bags, and baby seats on a wooden-wheeled cart. Thank you for your patience. We regret the inconvenience. And don't forget to fill out our customer satisfaction surveys!

We had taken Daisy to a fringe of green just outside one of the gates. But as the hour wore on, nature's call became more insistent. We all became more exhausted, and slightly cranky. Daisy may have nicely encapsulated our reactions. She deftly deposited a couple more morsels, softly, onto the hard, smooth floor of the concourse that world travelers traverse. Once more, they were bagged and disposed of.

We did not have to spend ten minutes the next day filling out an airline or airport customer satisfaction survey. Daisy had already registered a kind of two-star rating on the concourse floor.

AND THEN BACK HOME

The next morning, we resumed our walks with Daisy and decided to stop at a smoothie shop on our route. Caroline went in, I stayed outside, and Daisy was at my shoes, looking longingly through the window at the person she loves most in this world, and at a refreshment so favored and usually forbidden she might have wondered how fortune had set it just out of licking range.

I tried to distract her with footwork and songs. Daisy held her stance, and a steely, unflinching focus on the billows and sprays of pink, white, cherry red, and tangerine.

And then the door of the smoothie shop opened. Out stepped five high school girls from Winnipeg, in town on a school tour. They began to gush over Daisy, who decamped from her post where she'd been gazing at smoothies, which would be denied her, to a place next to them where she was bestowed with pats, rubs, giggles, and cooing. "What a cute dog! What a sweetie! What a *sweeeeetheart*!"

"She's heard that all before," I told them, and they told Caroline and me about their travels, what they'd seen, what they would see, and what they wished to see, as Daisy sprinted up toward their open hands for more pats.

A few minutes later, we were walking along the river and Daisy sprang from our route to bound, leap, and earn pats from a couple of tourists who turned out to be from Ireland. They filled us in a bit on their lives, and we offered a few suggestions about what they might want to see and where to go. Daisy frolicked between their outstretched arms. She reminded us that morning, as she does on so many, how our running mates can help us to notice those who are right in front of us, and to see those smiles that can help shine light into our lives.

And, oh, we returned to our apartment, turned a corner into the kitchen, and saw a white fluff boulder *plop!* at rest in the sink. Gato Blanco had somehow vaulted from the floor onto a counter that was supposed to be too high even for Tinker Bell to fly onto. Then he lowered himself into the sink. How? When? Why? *How?* What combination of cheetah or puma hydraulics, inherited from ancient forebears, had enabled Gato to make such a leap of fur? What aerodynamics? If we could see how Gato managed to hop into the sky and thus into the kitchen sink, it might reveal a whole new form of propulsion for the planet.

BAGEL'S BURIED TREASURE

I don't think we quite knew the extent of Bagel's mining enterprise until a recent cleaning of her cage. A small dig into her squishy, many-hued precincts revealed scores of orange and russet food nuggets, buried like time capsules in and under the crinkles of her spongy paper piazza.

You have to wonder: What might she know? What does she sense? Does Bagel possess a sharpened Rodentia-nurtured awareness of doom as she scurries on her wheel? Is she hoarding—or preparing? Are her food reserves the fruits of toil, spurred by misplaced panic, or merely intelligent groundwork for some future event that we, poor two-legged humans, cannot perceive?

If I ever hear winds whip and emergency horns blare, I might tell our family, "Okay, everybody! Grab Daisy and Gato, and let's all ride this out in Bagel's mine shaft!"

GATO AND THE NOVELIST

I was interviewing a novelist who is a superb writer, but unaccustomed to interviews. There were stops, starts, uhms, and uncertainties. Meanwhile, Gato Blanco had moved under the corner of the broadcast table, preparing to leap onto the top and saunter over to the microphone to offer his own insights. Except I'd recently placed a tray on that spot to hold books. Gato's runway was occupied. I angled my chair slightly for him to leap into my lap as I continued to listen to the author and offer questions. Gato clambered on. He nudged my chin with the top of his head. I began to stifle a sneeze from sniffing in a cloud of his fluff. The move to take a hand from holding Gato in place to put those fingers just under my nose gave him the opening he craved. Gato nudged the microphone stand with his soft pink nose. The author, our producer, our editor, and I all heard the scraping. Then he put his nose against the microphone.

There was a springy *thunk* of cat's nose on foam. The

author halted. Our producer said, "Hold up . . ." Gato decided he liked how the slick pink of his nose felt against the squishy gray foam of the microphone and pushed it again—once, twice, three times more.

"Sorry, it's our cat," I explained. "Gato Blanco. He only interrupts the best authors." I offered a few names.

The novelist laughed. "How cute! How is he? Tell him thank you for me. I don't feel so nervous now," she said, and indeed, Gato's unscheduled appearance seemed to lend her a little more comfort and confidence, sharpened her answers, and helped her relax. She had joined an accomplished circle: novelists, political figures, and artists whom Gato Blanco wanted to hear and chose to join. The interview went on, but better. I moved Gato to a spot by my feet, and he sauntered off to his next stop, as if to acknowledge, "My work here is done."

POETIC POOCH

Oh, and Daisy writes haiku. A number have even become popular on social media. There are people who have no interest in anything I have to say on those platforms but look forward to a new haiku from Daisy Richard Simone (the flourish of the added *e* is in her *nom de plume*), who expresses her observations in that ancient Japanese poetic discipline that captures, in a composition of five, seven, and five syllables, insights that are at once universal and unique.

Such as: How does a dog decide on long morning walks where to pause to raise a leg in relief? Daisy illuminates her deliberative process:

> *Not here. Sniff! Not there*
> *Some other dog once went there*
> *Here. Right here. Yes! Ahhh!*

And yes, like Proust recalling his life from the crumb of a madeleine, Daisy writes of what she knows. Right here! Yes! Ahhh! Pure relief. And pure poetry.

She has also written in contemplation after walks she considered to be too short, for her and for us. She takes up her poetic voice to ask—

> *Why the rush rush rush?*
> *You have got to stop and sniff*
> *Who has gone before*

There has been some speculation on those social media platforms, which seethe with so much misinformation and wrath, that I must somehow be implicated in these haiku. Daisy, after all (and I say this only in the clinical, zoological sense), is a *Canis familiaris*, i.e., a dog.

To which I can only say, "Daisy is a French poodle. They are known for their intelligence, hunting prowess, and elegant deportment, all of which promote her poetic skills. Or as Daisy writes of another popular breed:

> *French bulldogs are not*
> *Can they read Proust? Sing Piaf?*
> *Poodles can and do*

Daisy, for her part, is sometimes accused of allowing a "two-legger" to appropriate her poetic gifts to express themselves, sub rosa, on topics of popular discourse. But any survey of Daisy's poetic oeuvre will confirm that she expresses herself on the most pressing concerns in her quotidian world. Such as this Sartre-style contemplation:

> *Did I eat breakfast?*
> *An existential question*
> *I eat. I eat more*

The French component of being a French poodle is clearly a recurrent theme in Daisy's poetic canon. It is sometimes expressed in frank nationalistic exasperation:

> *American dogs!*
> *They yap like wolves at their food*
> *French poodles savor*

Daisy can also feel affronted by the multiplicity of breeder-concocted mixes who claim poodle attributes, even as they present themselves as some contemporary super-breed of canine:

> *Why labradoodle*
> *schnoodle, cockapoo, shih-poo*
> *When there is poodle?*

Why indeed, verily?

There are those who have assumed that Daisy's haiku are somehow inspired by Archy and Mehitabel, the cockroach and cat who claimed authorship of many columns and books also attributed to Don Marquis, a New York columnist of a century ago. His 1927 book, *archy and mehitabel* (all lowercase, because Archy, the cockroach, was too light in size to hold down the shift key for capital letters), is still widely read today. I read it in high school.

Of course all artists build on the contributions of previous practitioners of the craft. But Archy and Mehitabel wrote satire, that most perishable of dramatic forms. Daisy creates imperishable truths in seventeen syllables.

Like Orwell, Daisy is skeptical of pretentious contemporary clichés:

> *Don't call me a dog*
> *I am in the canine space*
> *Sounds more important*

Similarly, she sees through the plot clichés of current films in which dogs are a central character, writing—

> *Dog movies: so rote!*
> *Cute dog. Cute kids. Cue crisis*
> *Dog saves day. The end*

Daisy also questions the efficacy of robotic rug cleaners, with whom she feels in competition for small fragments of food that may spill from our cutlery. With manifest inspiration from Carl Sandburg's classic *Fog*, Daisy writes to Roomba—

You huff, puff, and wheeze
I pad on little dog feet
Scarf crumbs, and move on

Yet she is also gracious, as only Daisy can be, as when Argentina defeated France, 3-2, in the 2022 World Cup:

Les Bleus were great, but
Argentina was more great
I lift a leg high

Still, at the heart of Daisy's poetic life is the ambition of all great artists to place in our minds, for at least a moment of eternity, a truth that is undeniable and enduring. Here is what she sees in the first snow of a season:

Ah, fresh-fallen snow
So quiet, clean, immaculate
And I pee on it

I know what you may be wondering: How does Daisy, a French poodle, write haiku? Does she write in longhand (or long*paw*) with a Blackwing 602 soft lead pencil, of the kind Stephen Sondheim used so notably to author both the words and lyrics of his musicals? Does she write in pencil on onionskin paper, like Ernest Hemingway? Does she pick up a Montblanc Meisterstück fountain pen, like Salman Rushdie? Or, like Jane Austen, does Daisy provision her own ink and write haiku with a quill in a "quarto stationer's notebook bound with quarter-tanned sheep over boards sided with marbled paper"?

I will leave it to Daisy to tell us in her *Paris Review* interview ("The Art of Dog Haiku"). Let's not let curiosity about Daisy's methods distract us from the marvel of her work. I am always glad to see seventeen carefully crafted syllables from her appear on my desktop.

OPENING HER HEART

Elise has been working at a horse rescue barn. One day they got a call about two horses who had been abused and neglected. (Elise will get to tell her own story about this one day.) The horses had been impounded by local authorities. Our daughter and her rescue colleagues drove to pick them up and bring them back to the barn. The horses were weak, worn, and painfully thin. Elise and her crew held them and tried to care for them, but it soon became clear that at least one of them could not survive much longer. Elise stayed with him through a dark, cold night, holding the horse's head in her arms until a veterinarian could end his suffering.

Elise had lost loved ones, grandparents, relatives, and a young friend. But she did not have to be there at the moment they left. And now the life she was trying to hold on to and help through the night was slipping through her arms.

I was sad to hear about their night, and yet glad the mal-treated horse had at last, if only in his last moments, heard a voice of love, and been able to look into devoted eyes and feel the warm hold of a caring hug around his head. Our daughter's love for animals has always been a guiding and powerful part of her. We heard it in the laughter and care she had for her first numerous and indistinguishable fish and hermit crabs; through little Leona, who had encouraged her to crawl and nestled herself like a sentinel at the foot of her bed; through all the horses she rode and groomed and for whom she was a partner in shows; through Bagel, who hummed along on the wheel in her room each night, and had to be yanked loose from the glue of that rat trap beneath our stove; and through the constancy of Daisy. Our daughter's devotion to animals had opened her heart, and each animal has helped her heart to grow into a furnace of love.

TEAM REUNION

Daisy seemed glum when our older daughter left for college. She was accustomed to our duo of daughters. They would often sneak her away from one another, onto their laps or into their beds, and Daisy would bounce happily between them. But to have one of them not around suddenly, day after day, was bewildering to Daisy (and, for that matter, to us). It was one of those occasions when you do think, All right, maybe this is why words were invented. We'd hold Daisy and tell her, "Elise is going to college. She misses you, too. But she is studying important things. You know, math and science and French and equine therapy. She'll be back soon on her break, okay? In the meantime, there's FaceTime, okay?" Daisy's eyes would just continue to dampen and quiver.

One morning, Caroline and I rounded a corner on our morning walk with Daisy as two women stepped out of a downtown office building. The two young women happened to be, if I may put it this way, as visibly Asian as our daughters. Daisy began to leap. She tugged us along in a run. We pulled up to the two women as they reached the street, and Daisy reared up and seemed to fairly dance on her back legs, as if to sing out, "Our team is back! We're back!" Then, on seeing and sniffing that the two nice women were, in fact, strangers, or at least new friends, she seemed to deflate just a little. She still offered tickles and licks, but soon trotted ahead to finish our walk, now in a gray mood.

A few weeks later, Elise returned home for a weekend. Daisy sensed her coming down our hallway from the elevator, and began to leap to the height of the apartment's doorknob in expectation. We had to work around Daisy's jumps to open the door. "Elise! Baby!" Daisy began to run in circles, from Elise to Paulina, back to Elise, and then back again, as if to confirm, "You're here!" and then, "And you're here, too!" and then, "You're *still* here!" and then, "You too! Still here! We are *all* here!" We laughed and smiled as her circles stretched on, and were reminded, all over again, that bringing animals into our lives graces us with extraordinary moments that bring us to see how much we can mean to each other.

GATO'S DEVOTION

We open the door for a friend to depart one afternoon, and Gato makes a break for it. He lumbers down the hallway and comes to a rest in front of a neighbor's door, then looks up. Of course we wonder: Does someone have a stew on the stove? Is there a new cat in residence, or simply visiting? Or is a neighbor (and how much do we really know about them, anyway?) harboring a stockpile of cat treats, tuna, salmon, chicken, and cheese, behind their door, set to award them to that feline who sniffs them out?

We pause for a moment and lean forward to listen. It is a neighbor who performs, playing her piano and singing opera. Gato: Cat of the Arts.

WHAT WE LEARN

I don't want to risk a faintly scolding word to raise the question of what we might learn from the animals in our lives. After all, it's fine just to enjoy the ride. But I know that every cat, dog, fish, turtle, hamster, grasshopper, and other living thing we have brought into our family's lives has helped to lift us outside of ourselves. They remind us that caring for others can give our lives a sense of purpose. That care is at the core of what gives us life.

Our animals also call on us to cross boundaries to communicate, and to concoct a language between us that is utterly personal. Our communication with our running mates is in the tenor and intonation in our voices, the press of our hands and fingers, and the squeeze of our arms. We anticipate, infer, and translate. What do they want? Where are they going? What do they need? How can we help?

And our running mates can not only learn but unlearn, as we go along in life together. The latter skill can be as vital as the first. They can learn where to find food, and what time to show up, how to follow, hold up, hold back, and when to go forward, leap, clamber, lift up a paw, and how to fit into the crook of an arm. But they can also fast forget and forgive if we forget to feed or walk with them at an accustomed time, or turn away from their heart-tugging entreaties for food or comfort. They lick their wounds, don't hold grudges, and come back for more with us.

They are utterly sincere. I suppose that is a virtue, if not always a comfort. Our animals do not tell us we look good when we don't, or, for that matter, when we do, or that we're brilliant or interesting. They remind us that really, our looks or smarts don't matter to them, and neither do money, achievements, titles, medals, trophies, or attainments. They ask us just to be there.

And of course, knowing as we do that their lives, and our time together, will be compact and finite can prompt us to realize that all our time together is short, cherished, and to be packed with love and joy. We help one another enjoy the journey.

PUTTING IT TOGETHER

We have never been apart from animals. Some of the earliest images we humans made of ourselves show the animals who were then apace with us. The people who made the paintings in the Lascaux caves of southwestern France etched the forms of deer, horses, and aurochs alongside human beings. Many of the animals might have been targets for food and hide (and to be sure, many humans might have been prey for some of the animals). But the creatures shown leaping and sprinting seem also to have been regarded as our running mates some seventeen thousand years ago.

There are surviving bronze sculptures of cats from 600 BC in ancient Egypt, where they were considered conveyors of good fortune. They were bejeweled, venerated, and often buried alongside nobles who bade these cats to see them on their way to a hereafter. Running mates into eternity.

Artists have been picturing animals in their works for centuries, as we're all travelers in this same world. As youngsters, we read about animals who are artfully incarnated with what we take to be human traits. They are often lovingly imagined, as they are with Winnie-the-Pooh and Tigger, Paddington Bear, and Kenneth Grahame's Mr. Toad, who reminds us in *The Wind in the Willows* that "independence is all very well, but we animals never allow our friends to make fools of themselves beyond a certain limit." And E. B. White's Charlotte, the spider who may deftly and forthrightly introduce us to our first awareness of mortality, and the fleeting gift of grace. "After all, what's a life, anyway?" she asks. "A spider's life can't help being something of a mess, with all this trapping and eating flies. By helping you, perhaps I was trying to lift up my life a trifle. Heaven knows anyone's life can stand a little of that."

Even works not known for being sentimental use the characters of animals to vivify what we think of as human traits. When a famously tough-minded thinker like George Orwell set out to write a hard-nosed parable of Soviet totalitarianism, he gave voices to pigs in *Animal Farm*. You may think you know all about Stalin and Trotsky, but it's hard to disregard Snowball and Napoleon. We cheer to read of Kipling's mongoose, Rikki-Tikki-Tavi, and Jack London's wolf dog, White Fang, animals who, in crisis, choose to protect their humans as they would their family.

Our family has been fortunate to stand in the Prado Museum in front of *Las Meninas*, the 1656 painting by Diego Velázquez. It seems to show a palace room in which five-year-old Margaret Theresa of Spain is surrounded by figures of her court and a dog. The painting is often most noted because the artist includes himself, peering around the canvas he is painting, and also paints in a mirror in which the king and queen are shown, beholding their daughter.

But I've seen children, and not just children, drawn to look at the dog who is at rest in the foreground. The Spanish mastiff seems unsurprised and calm. He seems to look away from the gaze of all others, and we may wonder where. There is a playful, pink-slippered foot of a court jester on his backside. The dog would see Margaret Theresa as a little girl and playmate, not as a princess.

Some art historians have observed that he seems obedient and well trained. I suppose he would be, as part of a royal household. But I find myself thinking that this big brown dog may simply be at ease in these surroundings, amid all this bustle, with attendants, courtiers, and chaperones so busily coming and going. This dog, seen by so many over time, is at one with the humans all around him. He has companionship and purpose in his life, and lends people some of his joy and calm. That's the bargain we have with our animals.

Gustav Klimt shared his studio with many cats. Salvador Dalí often posed with his ocelot, whom he named Babou. Pierre Bonnard put his dachshunds into many of his paintings, having observed that the little dogs called out looks of tenderness and delight from those who held and beheld them. And it was a dachshund who seemed to pierce the heart of Pablo Picasso, a genius of an artist but a notably hard-edged man, "astonishingly creative, so intelligent and seductive," as his longtime romantic partner and muse, the painter Françoise Gilot, told the *Times of London*, but "also cruel, sadistic and merciless to others as well as himself."

Picasso, of course, painted many doves of peace, kept a pet owl named Ubu, and had many dogs, usually large breeds, a boxer, a Great Dane, and Afghan hounds. But when his friend David Douglas Duncan, the famed photographer, brought along a little dachshund named Lump on a visit to the artist's studio, La Californie, the little strutting wiener of a dog strolled into Picasso's esteem and never quite left.

"Lump, he's not a dog," Picasso told Duncan. "He's not a little man, he's somebody else." The photographer said Lump was the only dog he ever saw Picasso take into his arms. Lump made frequent appearances in Picasso's sketches, studies, and portraits, including fifteen panels for Picasso's studies for his own version of *Las Meninas*, usually as a note of comic charm.

And Picasso kept Lump near to him, even through a spinal surgery that left the little dog with a rolling gait that was "a bit like a drunken sailor," as Duncan phrased it. Artist and muse, man and dog, died within ten days of each other, in 1973.

Artists and writers often put animals into their stories and pictures to unfurl parts of their own hearts. They'd like the animals they've known or imagined, and often loved, to go on, and set off echoes in our lives. I guess that's why I find myself writing this, too.

ANOTHER DAY

I'll end on a morning of no particular consequence. Our oldest, Elise, was already at work at the horse rescue barn. She had sent an uninhibited message about a horse whose temperature she was taking and who couldn't, *ahhhem*, hold himself back.

She was not complaining. It is the work she chooses and loves.

Our youngest, Paulina, was getting ready for school. She was zipping and packing up all her books, papers, and snacks. Caroline had taken Daisy on her first walk of the day. Between sips of coffee, she heated Paulina's breakfast, served up a scoop for Daisy's first meal, packed lunch, called out reminders, and nourished our family in all ways.

Gato was on the counter again—the kitchen counter he is not supposed to be able to reach. Once, he might have waited to be alone, unseen, to try to scale it. But by now the lofty counter has become just another patch in his realm.

As Gato moved across last night's rinsed kitchen cutlery

with a light, Astaire-like step, Daisy had her head burrowed inside a tall, empty yogurt carton that Caroline had placed by her food bowl. Daisy nudged and licked whatever had managed to stay slicked to the sides of the container. She raised her ears and snout in time to notice me walk out of the kitchen, crinkling crackers in my hands. She followed the sprinkle of my crumb dust and gazed up at my hands with undimmable ardor, as if they held a light in the heavens.

Caroline left for the car to take Paulina to school. Daisy joined them, riding up front, sentry, lookout, and celebrity, so she would not disappoint fans at the other end waiting to see her. While they were away, I went up the stairs in our apartment to begin work, stopping first to note that Bagel, our hamster, had eaten last night's fresh snap pea. Or perhaps she had simply stored the bright green pea in her confetti-colored caverns. I briefly tried to imagine the riches of scraps she had stored in her remarkable subterrestrial garden of bright vegetable bits and brown food pellets.

Caroline and Daisy soon returned. I heard a new commotion in the kitchen. Daisy may have sensed a fresh opportunity for a snack to reward her labors on the trip to school and back. Surely Caroline was not going to eat breakfast on her own?

Gato Blanco strolled nearby as I began to work. He glanced left, glanced right, then bent his legs to spring to my side, and lowered his snout to examine whatever words I had managed to bring to the screen. Gato scrunched his face. His eyes seem to narrow and sharpen, as if he had become an especially exacting editor. And who would say that Gato had not?

Daisy barked at something. Perhaps she heard the woof of a dog outside. Or the trill of a bird on a limb nearby. Or the call of a neighbor or stranger as they made their way across the street below. Or children rolling and laughing on a path along the river. While I was much too fraught with thought, work, and busyness to pick up whatever worldly drama played outside. But Daisy's yaps and zest kicked me out of myself. She moved me to pause, look, and even wonder. Our animals have the power to make us hold up for a moment to try to see, really *see*, what we may have missed, or lost, or just not made room for in our minds and hearts. Such days of no particular consequence have come to mean everything to me.

POSTSCRIPT

Bagel, our hamster who had dodged fate in a cat's grasp and in the goo of a mousetrap, left us as this book went into production. We got to enjoy two years of her happy nocturnal scurrying and burrowing. We dug a hole for Bagel in a spot on the grounds of our building, under the gaze of a small garden angel. We planted the blunt end of her favorite toy—a stick with a small tufted heart—

directly above. Daisy looked on quietly. We said the Mourner's Kaddish (Bagel was her name, after all), and our multi-faith family offered personal memories and thanks for the way that she had brightened our lives. We leave all the sections in the book about Bagel in the present tense, as she is in our hearts.

ACKNOWLEDGMENTS

Amy Cherry sensed that there was a book about animals inside me that I always wanted to write, and gave me the chance to do it. My abiding thanks to her and her team at W. W. Norton.

Our family gives profound gratitude to Wayne Kabak for all the ways in which he looks out for us. He makes everything I do possible.

Thanks also to Maggie Feldman-Piltch and Erick Plascencia for bringing Cat, i.e., Gato Blanco, into our lives, and the three off-duty ballet dancers who thrust a little dog in Chelsea into our arms. And to S. R. O'Brien for holding on to so many of Daisy's haiku.

Thanks to the artist, Liana Finck.

Sarah Lucy Oliver, Evie Stone, Shannon Rhoades, Melissa Gray, Ed McNulty, Fernando Narro, Martin Patience, Daniel Hensel, Andrew Craig, Jacob Fenston, Dave Mistich, Elena Tworek, Gabe O'Connor, Michael Radcliffe, Samantha Balaban, and the staff of NPR's *Weekend Edition* earn special gratitude for allowing my feeling for animals to occasionally be heard on our program, and for enduring my various cat and dog interpretations.

And to Caroline, Elise, and Paulina: my loves, my life.